just

**THE
JOB**

H&

foo

& Tourism

*Also published in the **Just the Job!** series:*

just THE JOB — *Hospitality, food, travel & Tourism*

Lifetime Careers
WILTSHIRE

Hodder & Stoughton

A MEMBER OF THE HODDER HEADLINE GROUP

Just the Job! draws directly on the CLIPS careers information database developed and maintained by Lifetime Careers Wiltshire and used by almost every careers service in the UK. The database is revised annually using a rigorous update schedule and incorporates material collated through desk/telephone research and information provided by all the professional bodies, institutions and training bodies with responsibility for course accreditation and promotion of each career area.

ISBN 0 340 68789 4
First published 1997

Impression number	10	9	8	7	6	5	4	3	2	1
Year		2002	2001	2000	1999	1998	1997			

Printed in Great Britain for Hodder & Stoughton Educational, the educational publishing division of Hodder Headline Plc, 338 Euston Road, London NW1 3BH, by Cox & Wyman Ltd, Reading, Berkshire.

just THE JOB

CONTENTS

and health services. Emergency services. Inspecting
and advisory work. Professional work involving site
work or visits, etc. Miscellaneous.

JUST THE JOB!

The *Just the Job!* series ranges over the entire spectrum of occupations and is intended to generate job ideas and stretch horizons of interest and possibility, allowing you to explore families of jobs for which you might have appropriate ability and aptitude. Each *Just the Job!* book looks in detail at a popular area or type of work, covering:

- ways into work;
- essential qualifications;
- educational and training options;
- working conditions;
- progression routes;
- potential career portfolios.

The information given in *Just the Job!* books is detailed and carefully researched. Obvious bias is excluded to give an even-handed picture of the opportunities available, and course details and entry requirements are positively checked in an annual update cycle by a team of careers information specialists. The text is written in approachable, plain English, with a minimum of technical terms.

In Britain today, there is no longer the expectation of a career for life, but support has increased for life-long learning and the acquisition of skills which will help young and old to make sideways career moves – perhaps several times during a working life – as well as moving into work carrying higher levels of responsibility and reward. *Just the Job!* invites you to select an appropriate direction for your *own* career progression.

Educational and vocational qualifications

A level – Advanced level of the General Certificate of Education

AS level – Advanced Supplementary level of the General Certificate of Education (equivalent to half an A level)

BTEC – Business and Technology Education Council: awards qualifications such as BTEC First, BTEC National Certificate/Diploma, etc

GCSE – General Certificate of Secondary Education

GNVQ/GSVQs – General National Vocational Qualification/General Scottish Vocational Qualification: awarded at Foundation, Intermediate and Advanced levels by BTEC, City & Guilds of London Institute, Royal Society of Arts and SCOTVEC

HND/C – BTEC Higher National Diploma/Certificate

International Baccalaureate – recognised by all UK universities as equivalent to a minimum of two A levels

NVQ/SVQs – National/Scottish Vocational Qualifications: awarded by the National Council for Vocational Qualifications and the Scottish Vocational Education Council

SCE – Scottish Certificate of Education, at **Standard** Grade (equate directly with GCSEs: grades 1–3 in SCEs at Standard Grade are equivalent to GCSE grades A–C) and **Higher** Grade (equate with the academic level attained after one year of a two-year A level course: three to five Higher Grades are broadly equivalent to two to four A levels at grades A–E)

Vocational work-based credits	NVQ/SVQ level 1	NVQ/SVQ level 2	NVQ/SVQ level 3	NVQ/SVQ level 4
Vocational qualifications: *a mix of theory and practice*	Foundation GNVQ/GSVQ; BTEC First	Intermediate GNVQ/GSVQ	Advanced GNVQ/GSVQ; BTEC National Diploma/Certificate	BTEC Higher National Diploma/Certificate
Educational qualifications	GCSE/SCE Standard Grade pass grades	GCSE grades A–C; SCE Standard Grade levels 1–3	Two A levels; four Scottish Highers; Baccalaureate	University degree

INTRODUCTION

Hotelkeeping and catering is one of the biggest growth industries in Britain. Nearly one in ten people are employed throughout the UK in preparing and serving food and drink, and providing accommodation. There is a wide choice of training and qualifications available, either on-the-job or through the full- and part-time courses offered by many colleges.

There are thousands of establishments where hotelkeeping and catering skills are needed – hotels, restaurants, cafes, entertainment and holiday centres, fast-food outlets, pubs and winebars, contract catering organisations, motorway and roadside restaurants, hospitals, prisons, schools, colleges, factories and offices, trains, ships and planes, and the Armed Forces.

Once you have the skills and experience, it is possible – and quite common – to work abroad. Many large hotel groups have branches all over the world. Foreign language skills will help you, if you have ambitions to work overseas.

Would I like it?

- Hotel and catering is a **service industry**, and employees are at work when their customers are enjoying leisure.
- Many jobs involve a lot of contact with the public, and hotel and catering staff have to be smart, polite and helpful. Personal hygiene must be of a very high standard.
- Employers want reliable and hard-working staff. A large number of part-time staff are employed.
- The hours of work are not the usual nine-to-five, and are often long. They may include 'split shifts', which means covering two mealtimes, with a gap in between when you

are off duty. Hours may involve starting early or finishing late.

- If you work in a tourist area, you may have to take your own holidays out of season.
- The work is often demanding, with periods of intense pressure.

Wages in the catering industry

The catering industry has not been noted for paying high wages in the past, especially for those jobs which are basically unskilled or semi-skilled. However, pay and conditions of employment for both unskilled and craft workers, and for supervisory workers/managers in the industry, have improved in recent years.

CATERING & HOSPITALITY MANAGEMENT

Providing food and accommodation for people is big business, and the industry as a whole is the third largest employer in the country. There are many opportunities for managers, and a wide range of places to work. There are various ways of training, from college courses starting from the basis of some GCSEs or an Intermediate GNVQ, to degree or HND courses.

Managers are employed by hotels, motels, guest-houses, restaurants, cafes, pubs, clubs and holiday camps. In some instances, accommodation is provided within the establishment. This can vary a lot in size, comfort and standard. Remember that you may not be paid as much if meals are provided and you are given somewhere to live.

Managers are also employed to run catering and accommodation services in such establishments as hospitals, college and university halls of residence, canteens (in schools, offices and factories), hospitals, in the Armed Forces and on ships, boats and planes. Increasingly, the catering in these places is undertaken by a firm of contract caterers, which may be a national concern, recruiting managers locally where the need arises. There are still a few instances where the catering and hospitality services are run on a non–profit–making basis, such as in residential care homes.

There are also opportunities abroad, especially for people with foreign language skills.

Management skills

Being a manager can mean a lot of different things, of course. The general manager of a 500-bed hotel in London would be doing a very different job from an assistant manager in a 20-bed hotel in a small town. Like managers in all sorts of businesses, catering and hospitality managers are involved with planning, organising, controlling and monitoring the running of the business in their charge.

Managers need:

- planning and organising ability;
- a very good understanding of food, drink and accommodation services;
- an interest in furnishings and decoration;
- social skills to build good relationships with residents and clients, and also with staff;
- the ability to stay calm;
- the ability to deal with committees and boards of management;
- marketing and selling abilities – hoteliers and caterers sell a *service*, just as banks, insurance companies, retailers, etc, do.

People skills

Catering and hospitality management relies heavily on *teamwork*, where employees and supervisory staff work well together in providing a service. Managers rely on their chefs, housekeepers, room attendants and receptionists. They must enjoy working with people. Besides the staff, there are of course the customers or 'guests' to deal with. However irritating or rude a guest may be, and despite any other problems in the hotel, the manager must always try to be courteous and pleasant.

Many hotels with large reception rooms and a sizeable body of catering and food service staff market their facilities and services, not only for social functions, but also to businesses, and to research and training bodies. These groups may wish to hire the premises for their meetings or conferences, with or without accommodation. The manager plays an important role in ensuring that conference attenders are properly catered for.

Lifestyle

Working in catering and hospitality management is not a nine-to-five job, even if you move into planning and administrative work for a large hotel company. Managers have to work when other people are relaxing – at evenings and weekends. Many hotels are at their busiest during the peak holiday season. Junior managers often work split shifts – a morning session and an evening session, with time off in the afternoon. It is the sort of job which becomes your life, and which can limit your social arrangements. Attending evening classes can be difficult, but having leisure time when the majority are at work can be a plus.

Even in hospitals, schools and similar establishments, weekend and evening work and early starts may be necessary. Meals have to be provided round the clock. Only perhaps in industrial and contract catering are ordinary working hours more common.

EDUCATION AND TRAINING

There are various ways of getting started on a management career.

Modern Apprenticeships are for school-leavers and college-leavers aged 16 and 17, and they offer a chance to gain skills and qualifications within a structured training programme. They last about three years and will lead to NVQs at least up to level 3 (equivalent to two A levels). This could lead on to higher-level craft, supervisory and managerial roles. Accelerated Modern Apprenticeships are for 18- and 19-year-olds leaving school or college and starting their careers.

Advanced GNVQ in Hospitality and Catering – this is a two-year full-time course, needing four GCSEs at grade C/Intermediate GNVQ.

BTEC Higher National Diploma (HND) in Hotel, Catering and Institutional Management – this is generally a three-year sandwich course. You should usually be eligible for a mandatory award. The minimum entry requirements are one A level/Advanced GNVQ with supporting GCSEs at grade C (or the equivalent). Your subjects should include one showing use of English and, preferably, science.

Degree courses – many universities and colleges run three- or four-year degree courses in hotel, catering and institutional management subjects. Minimum entry requirements are two A levels plus supporting GCSEs, or an Advanced GNVQ. Your subjects should include maths and English and, preferably, a science.

Part-time courses

A few colleges and universities offer the BTEC National and Higher National Diploma/Certificates and degree courses on a part-time or distance learning basis for people already employed in the industry. NVQs are an alternative route, entirely work-based or with the support of distance learning or college-based study. The other main route is through the Hotel and Catering International Management Association (HCIMA) qualifications:

HCIMA Professional Certificate – this is a qualification for people already working in the industry who want to go on to supervisory level work. To be able to enrol, you need to be working full-time in the industry or to have had at least two years' full-time experience. This experience can be in food and drink preparation and service, or accommodation services. You would also need to show previous relevant study, such as City & Guilds or BTEC First qualifications, or four GCSEs at grade

C, to prove that you can cope with the academic side of the course. The qualification can be taken part-time, by going to college for day or block release courses, or by studying on your own through distance learning.

HCIMA Professional Diploma – this takes one year on a full-time basis, two years as a sandwich course, or three years part-time. It is for people with the HCIMA Professional Certificate, a BTEC National Diploma or other, equivalent qualification. A programme of bridging studies may be necessary before starting the Diploma course, though not for holders of the Professional Certificate. People already working in managerial jobs in the industry, with no formal qualifications, may be accepted and gain some exemption through the Accreditation of Prior Learning scheme. Distance learning is also offered.

HCIMA and other postgraduate conversion courses for graduates

There are one-year courses suitable for graduates with degrees in non-catering subjects, such as business studies, who want to go into catering services or hotel management.

WORKING ABROAD

Some colleges and universities arrange exchange and placement schemes in Europe, and elsewhere, as part of their courses. Some HND and degree courses include time spent studying or working abroad.

Adults: note that maturity and previous experience may mean that stated entry requirements can be relaxed.

COOKING & FOOD PREPARATION

Cooking and food preparation are a vital part of one of the largest industries in Britain – the hotel and catering industry. Job opportunities have continued to expand, despite the recession of recent years. You can learn to cook on-the-job, but it takes time and study to learn the more exacting and specialised skills of the trade.

The catering industry

If you are preparing for work as a **cook** or a **chef**, you are entering a very varied industry. You could be employed in a hotel, restaurant, pub, motel, steak bar, fast-food operation or holiday camp. There are many other establishments which have catering sections and employ trained staff; for instance in air, rail and sea transport, the Armed Forces, factories, offices, hospitals, schools, colleges and universities. In fact, about a fifth of all cooks work in the catering services sector – hospitals, schools and colleges. The number directly employed by industrial and commercial firms for their staff canteens/restaurants has dropped. Increasingly, the work is contracted out. Contract catering is one of the most rapidly expanding sectors of the industry.

Cooking as a job is very different from cooking at home. In most types of professional cooking, you cook for far larger numbers, using techniques and equipment which are different from the ones in your own kitchen. In a fast-food restaurant or snack bar, a **call-order cook** prepares individual meals as customers come in and order them. However, in a traditional hotel or restaurant, one **cook** may well be responsible for only part of a complete meal, perhaps sauces or pastries. **Kitchen assistants** do routine work like preparing vegetables. In directors' dining rooms, one cook prepares the whole meal for small numbers.

For staff with good training and experience, there are many opportunities to work in posts of responsibility, to move from one sector of the industry to another and to work abroad. It is an industry with lots of scope for broadening your experience and developing your career.

What it takes

- There is a lot of heavy lifting, so you need to be fit.
- You are on your feet in a kitchen, always on the move and often in a hot steamy atmosphere. This can be pleasant on a cold day in February, but much less so when the temperature rises in summer.
- Many cooking jobs involve working early or late hours, though in some jobs (in school canteens, for instance) the hours of work are shorter and more regular.
- In commercial and industrial catering, people may eat at all times of the day, so shift and weekend working is often necessary. Your time off may be when others are at work, and you may be on duty more than once a day.

Hotels and restaurants
Cooks and chefs

This is a very large area of employment. New entrants start as trainees after leaving school or following a full-time college course. The rungs on the promotion ladder in a large kitchen are:

- trainee chef;
- commis chef or assistant chef;
- section chef or chef de partie;
- deputy head chef or sous chef;
- head chef or chef de cuisine.

The **commis chef**, who is learning the job, spends three to six months in each section until he or she has mastered all the skills of the kitchen. Each **section chef** is responsible for part of the kitchen work – e.g. sauces, soups and some main courses, pastry (breads, sweets and patisserie), preparing and cooking vegetables, and larder (preparing starters, cold meats, salads, dressings, etc). The heaviest jobs are in the vegetable and sauce sections, where lifting huge pots calls for stamina.

Of course, the **head chef** and **sous chef** must be skilled in all aspects of kitchen work. But the head chef in a big kitchen is at least as much a manager as a cook. He or she oversees the overall production of meals, plans the menus, manages the staff, orders supplies and controls the costs, whilst seeing that health and safety regulations are met.

Kitchen assistants

Kitchen assistants do the routine work of cleaning vegetables, stacking dishwashers, weighing ingredients and keeping the kitchen clean. Simple food preparation tasks may also come their way. It's a job for a reasonably strong, practical person who is a clean and tidy worker. Starting as a kitchen assistant is one way to begin a career as a chef, if you're prepared to train and study for your qualifications.

Fast-food outlets

The cooking in fast-food outlets is generally simpler, but you have to be organised and able to work at high speed. Menus usually include hamburgers, pizzas, simple grills, chips, salads and sandwiches. In the larger outlets, to avoid customers having to wait, much of the equipment is highly automated, including rotary grills and deep-fryers. There are strict controls over how long food is kept in heated cabinets.

Fast-food cooks may be referred to as **call–order cooks**. Training is mostly on-the-job, as the various fast-food chains have their own ways of preparing food, and your work can be accredited with NVQs at levels 1 and 2. (See next section.)

Catering services

In hospitals, schools, colleges, etc, there are jobs for trained cooks and chefs (either work- or college-trained) and kitchen assistants. Because the range and type of meals prepared do not always need as much skill as hotel or restaurant food, you may find a higher proportion of kitchen assistants and fewer cooks.

Contract catering

Contract caterers provide food for hospitals, boarding schools, conference centres, staff restaurants, cafeterias and so on. Nowadays, they are also employed by local authorities to provide the school meals service, meals for homes and hostels, the meals on wheels service, etc. Catering firms recruit large numbers of qualified chefs and kitchen assistants. Many contract caterers train their own chefs and cooks. It's a growth area.

Small-scale cooking

There are opportunities for cooks working on a smaller scale, preparing meals for directors' dining rooms, yachts, small pub restaurants, wine bars, wedding receptions, private dinner parties, etc: in other words, up-market cooking for small numbers. Although you could do this from a background of hotel/restaurant catering, or even home cooking, there is also the option of taking a private cookery course. It's a good opening for the mature entrant (as well as for younger people) and provides the opportunity for self-employment and freelance work.

Vegetarian catering

More and more people are becoming vegetarians, and the catering industry recognises this. There are courses in some colleges which allow you to specialise in vegetarian cookery, either totally or in part. The Vegetarian Society also offers a Cordon Vert Diploma Course on which you attend one-week intensive modules. Contact the Society for information on this and other vegetarian courses available (see Further Information section).

Patarasiri – commis chef

'I got teased a lot at home because I was always in the kitchen, helping with the cooking. I always liked trying something different, and drove my family mad when I didn't get the recipe exactly right!

Working in a restaurant is totally different from cooking at home. It is also different from when I was studying at college, doing a bit of everything. Here, I spend a long time working in each different section of the kitchen. At the moment, I am having to prepare the vegetables: it can be very tiring, chopping all day! I enjoyed it more when I was making sauces, as the work was more varied. I am looking forward to moving up the hierarchy to head chef, so I can eventually oversee all the jobs – and plan the menu.

Kitchen work is hot, steamy and hectic – but very satisfying when it all goes well. One good thing is that my French is improving, because of all the French terms used in cookery. This means I can almost understand the menus when I go to France!'

In many larger cities, there are specialist catering employment agencies at Employment Services offices for adults or those with some experience. There are also private employment agencies offering vacancies in the catering field.

TRAINING TO WORK IN COOKING AND FOOD PREPARATION

There are various ways of getting started in cooking. With the preparation of fast food or simple snacks, training is usually provided on-the-job. But for quality catering, formal training and recognised qualifications are very important.

Training for school-leavers

School-leavers can make a start in catering through a training in employment scheme taking up to two years. The exact training which is offered varies between employers, but you are advised to go for training that leads to National Vocational Qualifications at level 2 and possibly 3.

Modern Apprenticeships will be available in some parts of the country, involving around three years of work-based training, usually supported by distance or part-time college-based learning. The apprenticeships will lead to NVQs at level 3.

You can find training being offered by hotels and restaurants, contract caterers and institutional catering departments. The Armed Forces offer catering training of a particularly high standard, which is always acceptable to employers when you leave the services. Training through employment or within the armed services will give you the chance to learn from experienced cooks and chefs as you work alongside them, as well as through college courses.

If you want to cook in the really top hotels and restaurants, and perhaps be a famous chef yourself one day, you should try to get experience at the best establishments from an early stage by working in four- or five-star hotels or restaurants which are highly rated by the various guides and food critics. That's how people like Gary Rhodes and the Roux brothers got started.

There are no specific entry requirements for a career as a chef, although individual employers may set their own. A reasonable general education is usually all that is needed, plus enthusiasm and stamina.

Full-time college courses
The other way for either school-leavers or mature entrants to get started on a cooking career is by going to college full-time. There are courses leading to NVQs which last one to three or four years.

The City & Guilds Cook's Professional Certificate is still available at some further education colleges on a full- or part-time basis; this is concerned with cooking on a smaller scale.

Adults wishing to come into the catering industry as cooks or chefs may be able to train through a government training scheme. Ask at your local Employment Services or TEC office. Note that maturity and previous experience may mean that stated entry requirements can be relaxed.

FAST FOOD

In fast-food catering, the skills needed are best learned on-the-job. This does not mean a long training. Staff who work in a fast-food restaurant or take-away food shop need to learn how to do just a few straightforward tasks, but to do them well. You have to work at great speed, be well organised and be nice to the customers!

There are far more opportunities to work in self-service restaurants, snack bars and fast-food outlets, serving food like burgers, fish and chips, pizzas and kebabs, than there are in the more expensive restaurants and hotels.

You might have to . . .

- chop vegetables, and do other jobs which prepare food for cooking;
- use microwave ovens, chip fryers, grills, and perhaps pizza ovens and pressure deep-fryers;
- prepare simple meals and snacks such as hamburgers, pizzas, salads and sandwiches;
- display the prepared food in a tempting way;
- make and serve drinks;
- serve customers from behind a counter and sometimes wait on them;
- lay and clear tables;
- wash up;
- work out customers' bills, take money and give change;
- pack take-away meals.

Working conditions

■ Kitchens are often hot and noisy – can you cope with these conditions?

■ There may be some heavy lifting – of things like large cooking containers or bags of potatoes, and working all day (or evening) on your feet is physically tiring.

■ Catering machinery can be dangerous, so care must be taken and safety rules observed.

■ You may be expected to wear a uniform. This will probably be overalls and some kind of head covering if you are cooking. There may be a different uniform if you are serving food.

Working with people can be difficult as well as enjoyable. Customers can be rude or complaining, but you must always be polite and helpful, even if you started work at 6am, or are nearing the end of a late shift.

TRAINING AND QUALIFICATIONS

You don't normally need qualifications, but you must be clean, neat and tidy. You also need to be fit and healthy for many of the jobs. It's hard work, and there is often a lot of pressure when queues of customers build up. If your job involves taking money, you need to be able to work out bills and change quickly and accurately.

Most training is done on–the–job. In most larger fast-food outlets, you are moved between work stations so that you gain all the different skills necessary, and you don't suffer the boredom that comes with endlessly repeating the same simple task. You also might take more interest in the quality of the food produced for sale and in the good name of the establishment, if you have worked on both food preparation and serving the customers!

There could be a formal training programme, if you work in a fast-food outlet with special ways of doing things. Nowadays, the sort of skills you gain in food preparation, shallow and deep frying, grilling, boiling and the handling of catering equipment can count towards an NVQ in Preparing and Serving Food (Quick Service) at levels 1 and 2. This can include off-the-job training at a college or training centre.

You will also be assessed for your skills as a **food service assistant**, making up food orders, serving, table clearing, preparing bills and handling money, after a period of training on-the-job. This would also count towards Catering and Hospitality NVQs at levels 1 and 2 in Serving Food and Drink at a counter or table.

After further training and experience on-the-job, you can progress to NVQ level 3 in Supervision of Food Preparation and Cooking or Food and Drink Service.

Training in employment

If you are a school-leaver, don't forget that you can use your Youth Credits to pay for training, usually with an employer, perhaps through a Modern Apprenticeship. There is probably basic catering work you can do in your area, where you would gain valuable skills and experience – and qualifications. Your careers service or careers teacher at school will have details.

Adults can often go into this sort of work without previous experience or formal training. There may also be a government training scheme you can go on – enquire at the Jobcentre/ Employment Service.

PROSPECTS

A career in fast food can vary a great deal, depending on the sort of employer. If you are with a fast-food chain and keen to get on, there are opportunities for promotion to assistant supervisor, supervisor and, eventually, managerial jobs. Promotion can come quite quickly, and often goes to people who have practical experience of the work on the shop floor. In smaller, family-type businesses, prospects may be poor for non-family members. There may not be enough staff for supervisors to be needed. Pay tends to be rather low for the unskilled jobs.

FINDING A JOB

Most towns have a range of fast-food shops, cafes and snack bars. There are openings in fast food for both school-leavers and adults. Young people are often preferred, because they get on well with the young customers and because their wages are lower! Both part-time and full-time jobs are offered.

Vacancies are advertised quite frequently, as there is a high turnover of staff. Jobs are advertised in local papers. You can also enquire about vacancies at your local Jobcentre or careers service. Also, you could try writing to ask about vacancies or, in the case of small businesses, calling in. Don't drop in during the lunchtime rush, though! In the fast-food business, personal contacts can be the best way to find openings. A part-time or temporary job can lead on to full-time permanent employment.

SERVING FOOD & DRINK

Many people work as **food service assistants** or **bar staff** in Britain's growing number of medium-sized restaurants, cafes, pubs and fast-food outlets. These staff create the first (and often lasting) impression of the establishment. So, although you don't need formal qualifications for this work, you do have to provide a welcoming and efficient service.

In Britain, there are now around 100,000 restaurants, cafes and snackbars throughout the country. Whether the customer is having a break during their working day, or enjoying a social outing in the evening, it is important that the service assistants help to create a pleasant and relaxing atmosphere in which people can enjoy their food. If you have been kept waiting ages for your meal, or have been served in an offhand way, you aren't very likely to go to that restaurant again. The care with which food is served should reflect the work and attention which has gone into the preparation of the meal.

What it takes

- You must be clean, neat and tidy and wear suitable clothes (many food outlets provide their own uniform).
- You also have to be fit, as the job can involve a great deal of standing and lifting and carrying.
- Speed is very important.
- You need to have a polite and pleasant personality.
- You need a good memory for orders and faces.

■ You may need to be able to add up bills.

Food service assistant

The business of serving food differs between types of catering establishment.

In a roadside or urban fast-food outlet, snackbar, tea-shop, cafe or bistro or small restaurant, you would:

■ clean and lay tables;
■ prepare a tempting counter display;
■ take orders;
■ serve food;
■ prepare bills and take money;
■ clear tables;
■ help with some food preparation such as filling rolls, making salads, etc.

There is not much chance of promotion if you do this sort of work, unless you work for a large company which runs a formal training programme for their employees.

In a hotel or up-market restaurant, the work is more skilled. Here you would be trained to lay tables with the correct cutlery and glasses, all highly polished. You might have to show diners to their tables, hand round menus, describe the dishes available and return to take orders. People paying top prices want their food served attractively with the right sauces and accompaniments offered. They want a balance between friendliness and efficiency. You may learn how to serve things like flambé dishes, which require some or all of the cooking to be done at the table. You may also specialise in wines, an area which requires a good deal of knowledge.

There are also jobs for food service assistants in hospitals, factory canteens and in the transport industry, on trains, aboard ships and, of course, air stewards and stewardesses count food service among their skills.

Basic pay for food service staff (or waiters/waitresses if they are so called) is not usually very high, but tips and possibly free food can compensate.

There are part-time and full-time jobs available. Full-timers often do shift work in hotels and restaurants, or split shifts, which usually means that you work over two mealtimes, and take a break in between. This makes for a long day overall, but many people like the non-standard hours. Hours may be shorter or more regular in places which open only in the daytime for coffee, lunch and tea. Trained and experienced staff can get work on a casual basis at banquets and dinners, and seasonal jobs in holiday areas, including work abroad. A foreign language is often an advantage.

If you get proper training and experience, you could become a **restaurant manager/manageress**. In large restaurants and hotels there are intermediate stages of promotion, such as **station waiter/waitress** and **head waiter/waitress**. It would probably help a move to a higher position if you were prepared to gain NVQs in Food and Drink Service available at levels 1 to 4.

TRAINING

School-leavers can use their Youth Credits to purchase training, usually through an employer. Such training should offer considerable work experience and qualifications. Modern Apprenticeships are also available, leading to qualifications at NVQ level 3. Ask your local careers service or the Hospitality Training Foundation for details of training available in your area.

Both school-leavers and adults can go straight into a job as a food service assistant, and then be trained on-the-job, or possibly on day release to college.

There is a range of full- and part-time courses offered by colleges which can lead to National Vocational Qualifications in Catering and Hospitality from levels 1 to 3. Schools and colleges can also offer GNVQs in hospitality and catering at Foundation, Intermediate and Advanced levels. Check course details locally.

NVQs provide a ladder system of qualifications for people who have already received basic training. You are assessed on your ability to perform a task, however or wherever you learned to do it.

There are courses for **wine waiters** run by the Wine and Spirit Education Trust and the Academy of Food and Wine Service (see Further Information section).

Adults may be able to gain new skills and experience on a government training scheme. Ask at your local Jobcentre/ Employment Service.

Bar staff

Bar work is available in pubs, clubs, hotels, on trains and ships, in winebars, and so on.

Bar staff serve drinks and perhaps food. They also wash glasses, restock the shelves of the bar with drinks, snacks, etc, and keep the bar clean and tidy. Senior staff or managers check the till at the end of opening hours. If there isn't a cellarhand, bar staff may also change beer barrels and clean the pipes.

If you work in a bar, you have to deal with all sorts of people. Most of the customers are pleasant, friendly and amenable, but there can also be customers with a strange sense of humour, and those who are rude or impatient.

You need to be:

- at least 18 years old;
- able to handle money and give change;
- someone who enjoys working with people;
- a good listener, cheerful, polite, unflustered even when the bar is very busy;
- quick-working and efficient;
- tidy in appearance.

For some jobs you would be expected to dress particularly glamorously or smartly. Different pubs require different types of bar staff to some extent. Up-market city pubs with a smart clientele may expect a different type of barperson from the homely local, not only in dress but in manner too.

Many bar staff work part-time or shifts, to suit the opening hours and the level of business. Early morning starts are not likely, but late evenings and weekend shifts are. All-day opening of pubs is increasingly common, so the hours to be covered can be greater. There are usually good opportunities for *casual employment* in bar work, like standing in for people on holiday, or covering 'outside' bars for concerts, sporting events, agricultural fairs, etc.

Larger bars may have senior barperson jobs. Working in a bar is also a good background for managing or running your own pub – or other catering facility.

TRAINING

Training is usually given on-the-job by the pub's manager, tenant or owner, or by more experienced staff. This can count towards NVQs in Food and Drink Service at levels 1 to 4, and On-Licenced Premises Management levels 3 and 4. Modern Apprenticeships are now available for young people over the age of 18 working in bars and restaurants where alcohol is served. The Home Office is consulting over amendments to the licensing laws which would allow Modern Apprentices to work in licensed premises, under strict supervision.

HOTELS: RECEPTION & ACCOMMODATION

Lots of hard work goes on behind the scenes to make an hotel an attractive place to stay. Housekeeping staff make sure the rooms are clean, tidy, attractive and comfortable. The front of house staff (receptionists and porters) should create good first impressions by being efficient and helpful and giving a friendly welcome to guests. All staff need to enjoy meeting and helping people.

Front office and reception

The **hotel receptionist** is very important. A guest's opinion may depend on how they are first received. Guests are often tired and hungry, sometimes impatient, and any complaint will first be made to the receptionist.

Receptionists therefore need:

- a calm manner;
- pleasant disposition;
- good appearance is important;
- clear speech;
- an ability to get on with people.

Languages are very useful.

As well as receiving guests and taking bookings, many receptionists have to keep accounts and prepare bills at the end of a guest's stay. They must therefore be competent with figures and money, including exchange of foreign cash. In a small hotel, one or two receptionists may deal with all the reception and clerical work. Larger hotels have a **head receptionist** and other reception staff working shifts to cover most of the day and night. There may be separate staff to deal with the financial side of things. Most hotels now have computerised accounting and reservation systems, and receptionists may have to operate a computer terminal.

Alisa – hotel receptionist

‘ I wanted a job where I was dealing with the public but where I could also use my keyboard skills. The careers adviser suggested I look at a career in hotel and catering and so I went to college for a year to study for qualifications in hotel reception and front office skills. It was not easy to get a job afterwards, but the work experience I did at school gave me the edge over other candidates, as I had a clearer idea of what the work really involved.

I love the work I do, as it is so varied. I have to answer the phone, check train/bus times for guests, recommend what places they can visit locally, check guests in and make out their bills when they leave. In quiet periods (usually when I'm on a night shift), I have to catch up on correspondence. I'm usually too busy to be bored. I try very hard to remember guests' names. It's great when I do, as they then feel important and tend to chat to me for a bit. The contact with the guests is the best part of the job. I speak a bit of Spanish, which helps when we have foreign guests.

I never forget that I am probably the first member of the hotel staff that guests see, and even if I'm not in a particularly good mood, or if the guests themselves aren't very friendly, I still smile and welcome them to the hotel. ’

TRAINING

Training can be full-time, or through day release or training 'in-house' with a large employer. Most hotels don't employ under-18s as receptionists, because some maturity is needed. One route for under-18s is therefore to take a full-time course which can lead to an Intermediate or Advanced GNVQ in hospitality and catering, or NVQ levels 1 or 2 in Reception. It's possible to progress to levels 3 (supervisory) and 4 (management) with experience. Some courses require GCSE qualifications at specified grades in English language and mathematics. There are also some short, intensive, private hotel reception training courses.

It is not essential to take a specialist course; clerical training and experience of dealing with people could also be very acceptable.

Housekeeper

Housekeepers supervise accommodation services, organising the work of cleaners and room staff and overseeing everything necessary for the comfort of the guests.

A housekeeper needs:

- good organising ability;
- an understanding of how the hotel works;
- knowledge of decoration, furnishings, textiles and flower arranging;
- stamina – the work is active and housekeepers are on their feet a lot;
- the ability to deal tactfully with staff and with guests;
- to enjoy varied working hours;
- to live on the premises, for some jobs.

Large hotels may have **head housekeepers** with several **assistant housekeepers** working for them.

There are similar jobs in residential homes, schools, college halls of residence and hospitals, although the job title may be different (e.g. domestic bursar/superintendent).

TRAINING

Housekeeping training can be taken either as a full-time college course or on day release. Some employers offer their own in-house training. Housekeeping training leads to National Vocational Qualifications from levels 1 to 4. Higher National Diploma and degree courses in hotel and catering cover accommodation services management.

Training covers such subjects as the organisation of a housekeeping department, cleaning methods, interior decoration, pests, stores, care of furnishings, room preparation, room service, laundry and security.

You could consider studying for an Intermediate or an Advanced GNVQ in hospitality and catering, which includes accommodation services as part of the course.

Room attendant

Room attendants clean and prepare rooms for guests. This kind of work doesn't need qualifications. Training will be provided by your employer. It's a practical job where you are constantly on your feet. You need to be quick and thorough, with a pleasant, friendly manner, and to enjoy providing a service. The best way of finding a job is by contacting hotels in your area. Some local employers may run training programmes for school-leavers. NVQ at level 1 in Housekeeping is suitable for room attendants. Ask your local careers service for further information.

Porter and related jobs

These jobs include porters, messengers, pages and door staff. A small hotel may have just one **porter**, who helps guests by giving information about the hotel and the area, getting luggage to their room, making arrangements for a call in the morning and anything else required to make their stay pleasant. In a larger hotel, the porter may have assistants such as **messengers** and **pages** to run errands, luggage porters, and **door staff** to welcome guests, open car doors and summon taxis. Portering is a job for a mature person who enjoys meeting people and is tactful, methodical and efficient. Lifting and carrying is involved. Someone new to this type of work would usually start as a messenger or a luggage porter. The **head porter** in a big London hotel would be a very experienced worker. **Night porters** are often employed to greet and assist late arrivals.

Steven – porter

❝ I like the hustle and bustle of working in a hotel. There are always people coming and going. I started work as a trainee, and really enjoyed it as I met a lot of different people and felt I was helping them to enjoy themselves. I must have done OK, because the hotel took me on permanently once I'd finished the training.

I don't only carry guests' luggage, but also get taxis for them – or even run small errands sometimes. It's really good if they're pleased with what I've done for them, because they give me a tip. It helps if I smile and am polite, even if the bags are very heavy! The hotel I work in doubles as a conference centre, so I also get involved in moving furniture around and carrying videos or other equipment from one room to another.

I like wearing my uniform as it makes me feel very smart. It also means I can save money on not having to buy so many clothes of my own. I only pay a small amount for my meals as well – and it's good quality food!

The downside is that I have to work shifts, which means that sometimes I don't get to see my girlfriend as often as I would like, but that's the nature of the job! ❞

GETTING STARTED

Qualifications are not usually required. To get started, contact local hotels. There are NVQs available in Portering at level 1.

Adults: specialist employment offices in London and in various other towns, your nearest Employment Services Office or Adult Careers Guidance Service can help. The Jobcentre also has information on opportunities for gaining skills and experience through government schemes for adults.

ACCOMMODATION WARDEN

The job of **accommodation wardens** is to look after residential hostels, such as halls of residence for students, YMCA/YWCA hostels, types of holiday/leisure accommodation – in the main, places for young people to live and stay. Other opportunities for wardens involve responsibilities closer to social work, e.g. in hostels for individuals with specific needs.

Throughout Britain, there are a very large number of halls offering accommodation to students during the academic terms at *colleges and universities*. These buildings all require **wardens** who generally live on the premises. During the vacations, the rooms are let to conference members, delegates on short courses, former students or visitors to the region, so the warden is kept busy throughout the year.

The types of *holiday accommodation* where wardens are necessary include youth hostels, outdoor activity centres and campsites. Here, the work can involve contact with all age groups.

All the *hostels* run for single homeless people, former alcoholics and drug addicts, *community houses* for people with disabilities, and the *sheltered housing* for elderly people, need accommodation wardens present on the site. These types of hostels may be run by local councils, housing associations or charitable/voluntary organisations.

Most jobs involve 'living in', at least while you are on duty – and you may consider the accommodation which goes with the job as a perk. Many of the hostels for people pursuing leisure activities are located in attractive surroundings, such as the Brecon Beacons or the Lake District. Obviously, the emphasis of the work will vary greatly according to the type of accommodation provided and the people it caters for. But, generally, it's a job which involves a lot of different responsibilities.

The responsibilities include:

- housekeeping – seeing that rooms are kept clean, bed linen changed, etc;
- collecting money – seeing that rents or fees are paid;
- catering – organising meals, seeing to communal kitchens;
- welfare – keeping an eye on residents, making sure that they live together as harmoniously as possible, and dealing with any complaints.

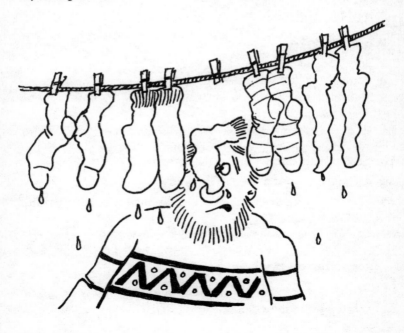

Work mainly involving the catering and housekeeping aspects of providing accommodation is often known as **catering services management**, and the previous section on catering and hospitality management gives more details.

If you work in a home or hostel for people with particular problems or needs, then the welfare aspect of the job will be the main one. You will get involved with your residents on an individual basis, and may spend a lot of your time helping them towards greater confidence and independence. For people with learning difficulties, this might mean teaching them how to cope with basic everyday tasks, like going shopping on their own, and cleaning and cooking for themselves. The warden in sheltered accommodation for elderly people has to be aware of the needs, health and safety, and general well-being of all the residents, and a nursing background is usually preferred.

What it takes

- good organising ability;
- confidence and self-reliance;
- ability to shrug off criticism if you have to make unpopular decisions;
- an approachable manner and a liking for working with people – but, in some jobs, you will also need an assertive manner at times;
- willingness to work unsocial hours;
- maturity – this isn't a job which you can do immediately on leaving school;
- previous experience and training in something like catering, youth and community work, social work or nursing, depending on the exact job.

No particular educational requirements are likely to be specified, but a good general education will help.

EMPLOYMENT

Positions as wardens of hostels are usually advertised locally in the newspapers and Jobcentres of the area. For jobs as accommodation wardens of outdoor pursuit or field study centres, youth hostels and recreation/leisure sites, look for advertisements in the quality newspapers and the *Times Educational Supplement*, which comes out on Fridays.

LICENSED RETAILING & THE PUB TRADE

Have you ever thought about working in a pub – or perhaps even running one of your own? There are over 65,000 pubs in Britain, plus a variety of other outlets where you need licensed retailing skills. Altogether, these inns and bars employ nearly half a million people. This section gives you some basic information about the industry, and the sort of life pub work involves.

Running a pub

Running a pub is as much a way of life as it is a job. The hours can be long and the work is frequently tiring. Because pubs open to cater for other people's leisure time, the working hours are often unsocial, although the introduction of all-day opening has enabled **licensees** and pub companies to organise staff time better.

What it takes

Being successful as a licensee requires all-round business ability as well as a good way with customers. The characteristic pub 'atmosphere' is created by both staff and customers, but each take their cue from the licensee, who must cultivate the popularity of the pub among regulars, tourists and many other types of customers.

Requirements for the job include:

- an understanding of financial management and cost controls;
- being sufficiently good as a personnel manager to bring out the best in the pub's team;
- catering and cellar management;
- marketing ability and bookkeeping are skills necessary to both control and develop the trade.

You also need to be able to convince a magistrate that you are a 'fit and proper person' to be granted a licence, and then prove it by understanding and complying with the licensing laws. There is also a range of other regulations and local by-laws which frequently have an impact upon those running licensed premises.

GETTING EXPERIENCE

The best advice for anyone considering running a pub is to gain some firsthand experience as a member of bar staff. This will give you a feel for the job and some insight into how well you interact with pub customers, sometimes coping with difficult situations. Additionally, experience of work in managing other people is useful, as in jobs where you need organisational abilities or provide a service to the public.

Potential managers and tenants need to demonstrate that they understand the work and have some background knowledge and business sense. For those few people who first enter the trade by buying a free house of their own, these qualifications are equally important. It is widely accepted that to enter the industry without completing some form of training course is foolhardy and can potentially lead to loss of your own money. The Qualifying Examination of the British Institute of Innkeeping or a NVQ at level 3 in On-Licensed Premises Supervisory Management are both useful and recognised qualifications. There are degree and Higher National Diploma courses in Hotel and Catering Management which include licensed retailing modules, and a degree in Licensed Retail Management awarded by the University of Wolverhampton.

Food
Providing food for pub customers is now an important and lucrative aspect of work in licensed retailing. Many pubs offer bar food both at lunchtime and during evening hours. Customers now expect to be able to buy at least a snack, if not a hot meal. Sometimes the provision for eating is elaborate, with specific restaurants or eating areas set aside within the bar. Breweries which own such pubs often appoint departmental managers to specialise in cooking, restaurant service and bar work. This can be true of the larger, independently owned public houses too.

Free houses
These are independently owned pubs which carry a wide range of beers and are not under the direct control of any one brewery. There are around 47,000 of these outlets throughout the UK. In Scotland the majority of pubs and small hotels are run as free houses.

It is quite easy to fall in love with the idea of owning a country free house, complete with a roaring log fire and happy locals, but there is a lot of hard work involved. For instance, simply negotiating the supply contracts can be a very tricky part of the economics, when you are trying to make a realistic return on investment. The owner is in fact responsible for all aspects of running the pub. In return, the owner takes all the profits, but a lot of capital or financial backing is needed in the first place. Free houses sell at anywhere between £60,000 and £1 million, depending on their size, proven sales and identified potential.

Managed houses
Nearly 19,000 managed houses are owned and operated by breweries, or by multiple pub companies, throughout the UK.

In these pubs the licensee is a manager and paid a salary, with additional bonuses linked to sales and profitability performance.

Most managers are given accommodation, but this is less likely in the lock-up pubs and bars found in town or city centres. Although this is not usual practice, some companies may ask potential managers to put up a security bond before taking over a pub.

It is unusual for a manager not to complete a training course before taking over his or her first pub. In large companies, the training is normally provided by the company's own internal training department, but in others the job is contracted to independent companies or to colleges of further education. The potential licensee then usually spends time acting as a relief manager whilst permanent licensees are on holiday. This provides very useful experience of the different styles and types of pubs.

To become a manager, it is not essential to be one of a couple, although it remains the case that the majority of positions for managers are for couples. Working as a pair helps share the responsibilities.

There is little or no age preference for appointing managers, although a growing number of companies like to appoint young couples from the age of 20 as assistant managers – perhaps after a spell working as a member of bar staff. This can frequently lead to first house manager appointments from around the age of 22–24. It is not unusual for couples to be appointed up to the age of 50. In some pubs, the experience they bring to the task is seen as an important attribute.

Working in the managed sector of the pub business appeals to:

■ those who want a career in the industry but lack the financial resources to invest in a lease, a tenancy or in the purchase of a free house;

- those who wish to gain managerial skills before using their own money to establish a business.

Management of a pub, which will include paid holidays and other company benefits, can prove more congenial than taking on sole responsibility for a licensed free house, for example. However, it's still hard work and the commitment required should not be underestimated.

If you are interested in a career in pub management you should write directly to breweries or pub companies giving details of your age and experience as well as family and other commitments. To improve your prospects, past attendance on training courses associated with licensed retailing, hospitality or catering should be stressed.

Tenancies and leases

There are a number of highly complicated ways in which breweries and some pub property companies rent their pubs on either short-term tenancy agreements or leases to individuals or companies, lasting twenty or so years. Nearly 33,000 pubs are run by tenant or lessee publicans. It is important to understand the full ramifications of signing such legal documents. Terms vary considerably, ranging from who has responsibility for outside signing and roof repairs, through to which products the tenant or lessee is obliged to buy from a specified brewery or drinks supplier. The lease company also nominates contractors from whom amusement or prize machines may be hired.

The tenant or lessee makes his or her own decisions about employment of staff, stock levels, catering menus and ensuring profit levels are maintained. In most instances there is a sizeable level of independence - provided the tenant or lessee fully understands and appreciates the trading relationship with their landlord.

Both leases and tenancies can be an attractive option for those wanting to run their own small business at a low capital cost. When taking over an existing pub, a new licensee is expected to purchase the stock and any fixtures and fittings which are deemed necessary.

As an outline guide, the capital needed for investment in a tenancy can range from about £12,000 upwards. Clearly the scale of the investment reflects the brewery or pub company's appreciation of the potential of the property.

If you are interested in a tenancy, you should apply directly to a company and ask for an interview. Often vacancies are advertised, and you can also apply to a firm of licensed property brokers. The details required will be similar to those asked for in applying for a position as a pub manager, but increasing emphasis is often placed on your construction of a business plan, and your having adequate capital resources. There is no legal age limit, apart from the 18-year-old threshold for serving any person in the bar area of licensed premises. Although maturity is often seen as a benefit, new tenants or lessees can be any age, provided they meet the brewery or pub company's qualifying criteria for a pub property.

Today, large brewing companies are tending to reduce the number of their tenanted pubs in favour of managed ones.

TRAINING

Increasingly, licensing magistrates question individuals on their level of training in considering their appropriateness to hold a licence. Many courses are provided by pub companies and breweries. Those which are valued nationwide are the training courses which lead to the British Institute of Innkeeping examinations.

There are a growing number of larger companies offering training programmes leading to the NVQ in Catering and Hospitality (On-Licensed Premises Supervisory Management) levels 3 and 4.

Bar staff

Bar staff do not have the same responsibilities as the licensee, but it is still a responsible job. At present, you need to be 18 years old to work in a bar area, and you need to be able to handle orders and payment confidently. You also need to enjoy working as part of a small team and be sufficiently flexible for the pub to be a relaxing place for customers, as well as profitable for the owner.

Your appearance matters, as do honesty, cheerfulness and politeness to customers. Some bar staff jobs require you to wear a uniform to convey a distinguishing style. Managers look for worldly-wise people, who can make conversation easily and contribute to an informal ambience.

Bar staff increasingly serve food as well as drinks. They wash glasses, restock shelves, keep the bar area clean and tidy, and may sometimes be expected to help with till checks, changing barrels and the cleaning of beer lines or to contribute ideas for interesting promotions. You must be prepared to deal with all types of customers and know the best way to handle occasional rudeness. You need to know your legal responsibilities on such matters as refusing to serve a customer who is under age or over the limit.

Most training is given on-the-job by the licensee, or by more experienced staff. Training can now lead to NVQs at levels 1 and 2 in Catering and Hospitality (Serving Food and Drink – Bar). Accelerated Modern Apprenticeships are available for 18–19 year olds, leading to NVQs at level 3. Under 18s may be able to find relevant training in exchange for Youth Credits. Ask your local careers service.

Many bar staff work part-time, at hours to suit them and the licensee. Full-timers may be asked to work split shifts where licensees have not taken full advantage of changes in the law allowing all-day trading. As well as in pubs, bar work is offered in clubs, hotels, wine bars, leisure centres and so on.

Wine bars

Wine bars are a specialist sector of licensed retailing. Whilst their growth probably peaked in the mid-1980s, they remain a regular feature of the high street scene. Like pubs, these bars may be privately owned, or part of a brewery or catering group.

Customers of a wine bar expect the staff to be more knowledgeable about wines than the equivalent staff of a pub. There are courses specialising in wines and the wine trade offered by the Wine and Spirit Education Trust and the Academy of Food and Wine Service.

Off-licences

Whilst all pubs and wine bars need an on-licence for the sale of alcohol for drinking either on or off the premises, an **off-licence** is restricted to sales of alcoholic drinks which will be consumed elsewhere. Most of the larger off-licence chains are owned by breweries or retail chains. Others are run as private businesses.

An off-licence store is required to observe permitted hours of sale. Evening opening is usual, except in shopping centres with little passing trade. The larger chains provide their own training courses for managers, whilst most small operators provide on-the-job training to ensure that a trainee manager understands legal obligations and company procedures. Knowledge of wines is particularly useful, and Wine and Spirit Education Trust qualifications may be gained through distance learning or by attending short courses.

Vacancies are advertised in *The Licensee and Morning Advertiser* (Thursday edition) and *The Publican* (weekly). For addresses of pub companies, breweries and off-licence chains see *Yellow Pages* or a list can be obtained from the Brewers and Licensed Retailers Association (see Further Information section).

JOBS IN THE FOOD INDUSTRY

The British food industry is big business, with many firms involved in processing what we eat. Food which passes through one or several stages of factory processing includes things like jam, bread, flour-based eatables, meat products (ham, sausages, pies), drinks (alcoholic and non-alcoholic), frozen vegetables, dairy products and chilled meals. There are job opportunities in production, testing and quality control, office work and management. For some of these jobs you need no particular exam passes, while for others a degree or equivalent qualification is required.

It is reckoned that a quarter of the average family's income is spent on food, a fact which makes food processing and marketing a very profitable, and very competitive, sector of industry. Count the number of advertisements for things you can eat or drink which are screened during an average evening's television viewing!

This is also an industry where extreme care has to be taken with all the processes that are used. Strict cleanliness is very important and every product batch has to be very carefully sampled and checked. The preparation, cooking and packaging of products is very closely supervised, and all companies, however large or small, must comply with the very strict regulations laid down in the 1990 Food Safety Act.

Food production jobs

Production is a term which covers a range of jobs, involving all the basic processes. Jobs include the preparation of food where this can't be done by machine (e.g. picking meat off chickens), loading and operating machines for mixing and preparing, and checking products. Most jobs are not very skilled and can be learned easily. They may be rather repetitive. Shift work is often necessary (some employers will therefore not employ young people) and pay can depend on how much work you get through in a certain number of hours (piecework).

Work conditions can vary from very pleasant to very hot (working with large ovens) or very cold (working in chilling or freezing processes). Protective clothing is usually provided and you must take great care with health and cleanliness. In a bread factory, for example, you may be paid not to come in if you have a cold or infection. With experience, promotion to more responsible supervising and quality control positions is possible.

Scientific jobs

These positions are covered more fully in a later section, on food science and technology. The qualifications required range from four GCSEs at grade C, or their equivalent, up to degree level. The tasks are concerned with checking and testing ingredients, products and processes, to ensure that the food tastes right and is safe to eat. There is also work involving the preparation and testing of new products and processes.

Management and office jobs

As in any other large division of industry, the food sector employs people in sales, marketing, accountancy, personnel, computing and general management. These jobs are much the same as in other industries, and the *Just the Job!* books on these occupations will tell you about the qualifications and training involved. Many larger firms recruit graduates to train for management. There are also clerical and secretarial jobs – again differing only in detail from those in other industries.

Small businesses

Food producing has become an industry of huge businesses dominated by giant firms like Unigate and United Biscuits. In addition, there are openings in the growing number of small firms making wholefood or traditional, high-quality products. Small-scale bakers, brewers, cheese makers and producers of many other kinds of food and drink have seen this opportunity and found a market for something different.

BAKING & CONFECTIONERY

Baking is an ancient craft, traditionally carried out by both men and women. It provides us with one of our basic foodstuffs, bread, as well as all sorts of delicious extras like buns, pastries, gateaux and cakes. Bakers can work anywhere, from huge factories to corner shops. The basic skills of the trade are taught in colleges, or by **master bakers** who have gained their expertise through years of work in the craft.

The bakery industry is based on three broad groups:

- large firms with automated plants which produce about one and a half million tonnes of bread and cakes for countrywide distribution annually;
- craft bakeries which have only a small workforce and which usually combine a bakery with a shop;
- bakeries in the large retail stores such as Tesco, Sainsbury and Safeway, where five or six bakers are employed to produce a full range of bread and cakes to sell over the counter.

For some time, it looked as though the enormous sliced bread factories were going to put the small baker out of business. However, recently, there has been a surge in demand for crusty fresh bread and wholemeal loaves. This customer interest has resulted in the large-plant bakers also offering a wider and improved range of products.

Jobs in the industry

Qualified bakers have lots of opportunities for work. In a bread factory, for instance, bakers can work as supervisors or foremen/women, research workers, test bakers (on quality control) and, with experience, as production or plant managers. In both small bakeries and large plants, there are opportunities to specialise in cake design and decoration, chocolate work and continental confectionery or patisserie work (gateaux, eclairs, etc). In small firms, trained bakers may have to produce anything from bread rolls to wedding cakes.

Some points to think about

- Large industrial bakeries often operate twenty-four hours a day, which means working night shifts and weekends.
- You may well be working as part of a team.

- You have to work to very high standards of hygiene.
- Small baking businesses start very early in the morning, to have fresh products ready to sell when the shop opens, including Saturdays. You have free time in the afternoons and some workers find that this is a bonus.
- Although the work does not require strength, you do need physical stamina.
- Many bakers would agree that there is great *job satisfaction* in making nutritious and attractive cakes, pastries, etc, from very simple starting materials.
- There is a great variety of activity in a craft bakery, but you do have to watch the clock carefully, so as not to singe the batches!
- You are on your feet all the time, often working in a hot atmosphere.

TRAINING

It is possible to work in a large plant as an operator or packer with on-the-job training. For the more skilled tasks, training is essential. This can either be through day or block release to college, or by taking a full-time course. Currently, there are a number of different training routes available.

You could work towards National Vocational Qualifications at NVQ level 2, or to level 3 in supervisory management or at technician level. These awards are made by City & Guilds, and also by the Hotel and Catering Training Company.

There are some further education colleges offering college diploma courses in bakery skills. BTEC National Diploma/Certificate courses for technicians in the bakery industry are still running, alongside courses now leading to an Advanced GNVQ in Manufacturing (Food Industry) which will eventually replace the BTEC National courses.

The Glasgow College of Food Technology offers a two-year full-time Higher National Diploma course in Baking Technology and Bakery Process Management. The National Baking School at South Bank University offers a three-year BSc degree course in Product Management which covers baking technology.

There are sometimes opportunities for young people to start gaining experience through employment with training. Your careers service will have details of the local training credit scheme.

Adults may find training opportunities available through Training for Work: contact your local Jobcentre for information.

BUTCHERY

The meat industry is a large business. We are familiar with the butcher's shop, but there are several other jobs which you could do working with meat. There are **abattoirs** where animals are slaughtered and prepared for the butchery processes. **Wholesale butchers** cut up and prepare meat for supermarkets and caterers. **Meat manufacturers** make prepared meat products such as pies, sausages and hams, and there are often **butchery departments** in large supermarkets. There is a lot to learn about meat preparation and presentation, and there are good training opportunities for new entrants.

Slaughterhouse work

Slaughterhouses or abattoirs employ staff to handle livestock before slaughter. They carry out the 'humane' killing of the animals, which are stunned before being slaughtered, and then they skin and prepare the carcasses for sale. There is also a lot of work involved in keeping instruments sharp and sterilised, and the slaughterhouse clean and hygienic. There are many rules and regulations to be observed in an abattoir – raw meat can easily become a carrier of disease.

Most abattoirs are quite large and are, in effect, meat-producing factories, where a percentage of the workforce may be doing butchery tasks, turning the carcasses into joints ready to cook. Some of the work can be heavy and tiring, and it is not for the squeamish.

Butchery

Butchers can work in wholesale butchery, in supermarkets or in specialist butchers' shops. Their work is a mixture of a craft (the ways of cutting up and preparing meat) and retailing (dealing with customers and running a shop).

Working in a butcher's shop requires a good knowledge of meat: customers often ask for advice on the choice of meat, and even for information on cooking particular joints. A shop with friendly, helpful staff is more likely to do well. Working in supermarkets and in wholesaling does not normally involve customer contact, and the work is rather more routine.

QUALIFICATIONS AND TRAINING

Educational qualifications are not normally required for entry to butchery or slaughterhouse work, although there are employers who may specify some GCSEs.

You need to be fit and healthy, as the work can be strenuous, with heavy lifting, and it usually means being on your feet all day.

Training is normally on-the-job, probably with day release to college. National Vocational Qualifications can be attained between NVQ levels 1 and 4, so qualifications are on offer for people working in butchery at all levels – from basic level to management. The Worshipful Company of Butchers offers some training scholarships (including opportunities for work experience abroad) to people of all ages who have had some experience of the trade. The University of Bristol runs a one-year postgraduate course which leads to an MSc in Meat Science.

Finding a job or training

One way to find work is to contact employers in your area and see if they are likely to have vacancies. There are also opportunities for young people to get started through employment with training. Your local careers service should have details of the opportunities available with training credits in modern apprenticeships. Adults may find training opportunities through Training for Work – further information about these schemes can be obtained from your local Jobcentre.

PROMOTION OPPORTUNITIES

In a slaughterhouse you can become a supervisor. Alternatively, you can move on to the management side, if you are prepared to work hard and take further qualifications, such as those offered by the Meat Training Council. In butchery, you can also do supervisory work, or run a shop or meat department in a supermarket.

There is also the job of **meat inspector**. This is very specialised work, involving the checking and certifying of meat (both home-produced and imported). Meat inspectors work for the Meat Hygiene Service, although a few are employed by large meat firms. It is possible to become a meat inspector either by qualifying as an environmental health officer, or by taking the exams of the Royal Society of Health while working in the meat trade.

FOOD SCIENCE & TECHNOLOGY

Food science and technology is an important part of Britain's huge food industry. Although it is already a highly competitive and very advanced industry, there are always processes to be improved, new products to be devised and new methods of preservation to be developed. Food scientists and technologists are degree holders; there are also opportunities for technicians with lower qualifications.

Feeding the population of the British Isles is a big and complex business. Most people's shopping bags nowadays contain items that have been frozen, chilled, freeze-dried, canned or bottled. A huge range of pre-prepared foods is available on the shelves of any supermarket. The availability of all these products depends on the work of food scientists and technologists. Fashions in food change like any others, and manufacturers compete to produce what the public wants. New techniques can occasionally be controversial. The present trend is for fewer chemical additives, so more natural ways of extending shelf-life are needed.

As well as working within the food manufacturing industry, food technologists and scientists are also employed in food retailing, environmental health and government departments, such as the Ministry of Agriculture, Fisheries and Food (MAFF).

The different specialisms

Food science is the study of all the basic theories and principles of producing, processing and storing food. **Food**

technology is the business of putting that knowledge to practical use. **Food engineering** is the branch of engineering concerned with these food operations, in particular the design of processes and equipment.

The divisions between food technology, food science and food engineering are flexible: a person specialising in one must possess some knowledge of the other two. It is possible to move from food science to technology and vice versa. **Food engineers**, however, must have a very strong engineering background, although they also work in food technology.

Food technologists and engineers may work in production, management, product and process development, quality control, and research and development in related fields. Supporting staff include **food technicians**. Food engineers may also be engaged in the design, installation and sale of food machinery and equipment.

Food scientists may work in research and development on materials and processes. They may also work in production and in quality control.

Both food scientists and technologists may find their way into marketing, technical sales or buying raw materials.

OPPORTUNITIES AND PROSPECTS

Food consumption in Britain is hardly likely to decline, so employment prospects for both young and mature entrants are good. Since food manufacture and processing methods are very varied, it is possible to specialise or to develop particular interests.

Food engineers and technologists are employed by manufacturers of equipment and/or packaging materials for the food industry. There are also openings in teaching and lecturing, in food retailing, in environmental health, in central and local government advisory services, in government research institutes, in industrial research associations and in international agencies. There are also some opportunities to work on projects in developing countries. A new area involves the introduction of modern techniques into large-scale catering. Graduate entrants to the industry can move into general management from scientific and technological work.

EDUCATION AND TRAINING

Graduate/technologist level

Most food scientists and technologists qualify by taking a full-time or sandwich degree course in food science, food technology or food manufacture. Some qualify first in another branch of science, such as chemistry, physics, biochemistry, bacteriology, microbiology or engineering. They then either take a postgraduate course in food science, food technology or engineering, or receive specialist training within the industry. Some sponsorships are available.

The normal minimum requirement for a degree course is five GCSEs at grade C (or equivalent) plus two A levels (preferably including chemistry). Three A levels are preferable for many courses. A relevant BTEC National Diploma/Certificate or Advanced GNVQ may also be acceptable.

The entry requirement for a BTEC Higher National Diploma is one A level, a BTEC National Diploma/Certificate or Advanced GNVQ. If taking the A level route, two maths and science subjects (one of which must be chemistry) should have been studied, and one of them passed. Appropriate HND course titles are Science (Food Science) and Science (Technology of Food).

Technician level

For entry to BTEC National Diploma and Certificate courses, or to Advanced GNVQ, four GCSEs at grade C are usually required. The GCSEs should include one subject which demonstrates use of English and two science subjects (preferably including mathematics). Entry to BTEC National/Advanced GNVQ is also possible following other relevant courses of further education (e.g. BTEC First Diploma or Intermediate GNVQ). There are also NVQs in Food and Drink Manufacturing Operations, which are practical qualifications and are open to people without GCSEs.

Adults: note that maturity and previous experience may mean that stated entry requirements can be relaxed.

HOME ECONOMIST

Home economists are professional advisers on food, nutrition, textiles and fabrics, clothing, and home management and design. They are concerned with people and their home environments, and must therefore understand people's physical, social and emotional needs, as well as their financial pressures. Home economists are likely to need qualifications ranging from a few GCSEs to a degree.

Most jobs for home economists occur in the food, textile and related industries. Opportunities also exist with the fuel industries and various advisory boards. Teaching posts are widespread. A home economist may also work in market research, public relations and social work. Some posts involve a lot of travel.

Employers of home economists include:

- gas and electricity companies;
- advisory boards for particular foods (e.g. meat, flour);
- major manufacturers of food products, fashion and textiles, domestic equipment and electrical appliances;
- retailing organisations, who employ home economists in product development and evaluation, consumer liaison, promotional work, staff training, management and personnel work;
- state and private schools and colleges, who employ home economics teachers mainly in technology departments;
- local authorities which run consumer advice centres, mainly in larger towns;

- the media, notably women's magazines and specialist periodicals.

Types of work for home economists
Product development
In manufacturing industries and retail outlets, home economists are employed as a link between the organisation and the consumer of its product, whether that is a tin of baked beans or a tumble-drier. They work with colleagues in product development, production, marketing, public relations and advertising – using their expertise to help the organisation get the product right for the market. With current concerns about our eating habits, including the increasing use of convenience foods, home economists have a particularly useful role to play.

Consumer advisory services
Home economists also deal with consumers. This may be by personal contact in consumers' own homes, in local authority consumer advice centres, trading standards departments or in retail shops where they would, for instance, demonstrate and give advice on the best way to use a product. Some home economists may be involved in correspondence with consumers – those writing in with complaints or queries about a product. Manufacturers of food products often offer an advisory service to customers, through which they can obtain advice, nutritional information and recipes.

Communications and journalism
Home economists can work in advertising, public relations, television and radio. In newspaper and magazine journalism, there are opportunities both in publications aimed at the general public and also in specialist trade, professional and technical publications. Home economists working on the latter are concerned with fact-finding, assessing products, writing reports and

articles, and answering specialist enquiries. On papers and magazines for the public (and especially women's magazines), the work may be rather different. Here, home economists can make use of creative ideas and skills (with food, fabrics, home furnishings, etc), using both their writing skills and practical skills in preparing items for photography. Besides being actually employed on the staff of a paper or magazine, there is scope for freelance writing. Specialised book production is another area with similar opportunities.

Advertising and promotions

On the advertising and promotions side, home economists concerned with launching a new product might organise demonstrations nationally or in selected areas. They might also organise competitions, and various promotional events in suitable stores and at exhibitions, etc. Press relations is also part of the work – arranging meetings with journalists who might be persuaded to mention the product favourably in their columns. Preparing food to be photographed for promotional material is a specialism in its own right.

Technical research and development

Home economists in manufacturing industries can use their expertise in the development of a new product. They work closely with other professionals such as industrial designers, physicists, chemists, food and textile technologists, marketing experts, etc. They are involved in testing the product, and the work is largely laboratory-based.

Community services

There are some opportunities with public social services and charitable organisations for home economists to work with members of the public such as the elderly or disabled, those on low incomes, families with difficulties, and so on. They advise on making the best of limited resources and on other aspects of home and family care. In some areas, they may organise a home-carer service, or meals-on-wheels volunteers (though people with backgrounds other than home economics may also do this sort of work). There are also opportunities in developing countries, for those with a special interest in food and nutrition, to work on self-help education programmes, etc.

Teaching

Teaching employs a lot of people interested in home economics, but it is important to note that the training of teachers for schools is generally different from that of non-teaching home economists. Often, teachers in schools specialise during training in either food and nutrition or dress and fabrics, though they may still teach both subjects on occasions.

To be able to teach in schools, you need a degree-level qualification, plus special training in teaching skills. Usually, this will mean a BEd degree specialising in home economics, though it would also be possible to follow a BA or BSc in a home economics subject with a postgraduate teaching course. You will normally need at least two A levels/Advanced GNVQ plus supporting GCSEs at grade C. Subjects must include English and mathematics. Training colleges generally expect BEd students to have an A level in home economics amongst their qualifications.

In further education colleges, teachers may come from differing backgrounds. Those who will be training future home economists are likely to have a diploma/degree, plus several years' experience as professional home economists themselves. Those teaching GCSE classes, however, might have the same background as a schoolteacher. There are also opportunities for part-time and sessional work with adults taking day and evening classes. Rural home economics teaching in colleges of agriculture is another possibility. It is not compulsory to be a qualified teacher for any type of teaching in further education, though training (either in-service or pre-entry) is increasingly expected.

Which school subjects?

At school, it is important to take sciences (either a balanced science programme or chemistry and biology) in preparation for careers in home economics. You will normally need at least one science GCSE at grade C, or equivalent, and it is a great advantage to have science A levels too. Indeed, for some degrees in home economics subjects, two science A levels are required.

Home economics subjects are, of course, very valuable too. Enjoyment of these at school often sparks off the interest in a home economics career. Intending teachers, especially, are advised to take GCSE and A level in a home economics subject – though not at the expense of important sciences. If, perhaps for timetabling reasons, you have not been able to take home economics at school, you should still be able to make a career in home economics – although probably not in schoolteaching.

Kim – home economist

‘ I knew I wanted to do home economics as a degree. I'd done it at GCSE level and wanted to continue to A level, but was advised it would be more useful to take science A levels (or you could take an Advanced GNVQ now). There seemed so much I could do after my degree – the choice was vast. I decided to specialise in the food industry, as I'd like eventually to work for a women's magazine, inventing recipes, testing new products and organising all that wonderful food to be photographed attractively!

At the moment I am working for a large food manufacturer. I have to look at new or existing products from the consumer's point of view. It's up to me and the team I work with to decide whether the products are good quality and good value for money. We also check that the instructions are clear enough on product labels. The best part of the job is when I get to test the food. Luckily there is no danger of me getting fat, as I'm kept far too busy for that.

I need to be good at English, as I have to write many quite complicated reports. I have to cope with a fair degree of statistical information too, and I find that quite hard.

I know it won't be easy to get a job on a magazine. If I don't succeed, I might try my hand at freelance writing in this field and see where that leads me.

TRAINING COURSES IN HOME ECONOMICS

It is very desirable, though not essential, to take full-time training in home economics. Training courses below degree level are run by the Business and Technology Education Council (BTEC).

BTEC National Diploma in Home Economics – a two-year full-time course requiring four GCSEs at grade C or equivalent for entry, subjects to include English and a science.

BTEC Higher National Diploma – a two-year full-time course for those having either the BTEC National Diploma, or one, and very possibly two, A levels/Advanced GNVQ and four GCSEs at grade C or equivalent, including English and a science. Students can expect to receive a mandatory award from their local education authority.

Degrees – these are offered at some institutions of higher education. Specialisation varies greatly from course to course, so read prospectuses carefully. At least two A levels (or equivalent) are required, and science subjects may be demanded. Again, a mandatory award can be expected.

Related courses – various courses with a home economics type of content are run by colleges of further education in subjects like housekeeping, home management and family care. These do not normally provide entry to the professional careers described in this section, but can make use of similar interests.

Adults: there is no reason why adults should not train as home economists and take up the full range of employment. There are jobs in which maturity may be seen as an advantage – e.g. working face-to-face with consumers, social services clients, etc.

WANT TO TRAVEL?

Do you want a job which gives you the chance to travel and to get out and about? It probably sounds much more exciting and interesting than a job in a factory, office or shop. But what do you *mean* by travel?

Do you want to travel around your town, within your county, all round Britain, or overseas? A bus driver and a geologist both travel as part of their work, but they travel on a very different scale. The bus driver may only tour around the local area. The geologist may spend several years abroad.

Do you want a job which takes you away for days, weeks or even months at a time? Or would you prefer a job where you usually come home at the end of the day?

How much travelling would you want to do? Do you see yourself travelling most of the time – perhaps in a transport job, as an air steward, lorry driver, or merchant seaman? Or do you view travelling only as the means to getting somewhere to do a job, like a telephone engineer or a district nurse?

What it means to travel in a job

There are some things you might enjoy ... and some you might not:

■ You will see new places and meet new people.

- Making friends can be awkward if you're always on the move, especially if you work shifts, or if you are away for considerable lengths of time.
- Your work may be less supervised than in an office job.
- It may be difficult to keep up hobbies and interests – for instance, being in a sports team.
- There can be perks such as a company car, petrol allowance, an expense account, and extra pay for unsocial hours.
- Driving, especially in heavy traffic, can be stressful.
- Travel may mean long hours, jetlag and eating out all the time.

What about when you're older?

Do you think you'll always want a job involving travel? Or might things be different when you're 22? 25? 40? 55? Some jobs can be done on either a travelling or a non-travelling basis, but others – and specially jobs in transportation – inevitably involve travel.

You may feel travel is less attractive when you are older, or if you get married and have a family, or when you've simply had enough of it! So it's a good idea to have some skills or training which you can use in more settled work. Otherwise, you will have to retrain for a new kind of job at some stage. The need to retrain faces a lot of people coming out of the Forces or the merchant navy, for instance.

Of course, these days, many people change direction during their working lives, as circumstances and opportunities alter. The days of working for forty years with the same company have largely gone. So, this situation is certainly not unique to jobs which involve travel.

Some ideas to get you started

This section shows you the very wide range of jobs where there is a need to travel. It cannot include *all* the jobs there are! But,

it should give you some ideas. If any of these suggestions appeal to you, the relevant title in the *Just the Job!* series will help you to find out more about that particular type of work.

Travel and transport jobs

These jobs involve travel most of the time. Some can be done on a local basis. Some take you all over the country, or even the world. If this group of jobs interests you, think carefully about the probable effects on your lifestyle which are mentioned above.

Please note that not all of the jobs are suitable for school-leavers, as there are age restrictions.

■ aeroplane or helicopter pilot

- Army, Royal Air Force, Royal Navy
- bus/coach driver
- cabin crew on planes, ships, coaches
- chauffeur
- courier
- delivery work
- furniture removals
- lorry/van driver
- merchant navy, including passenger services on board ship – catering, hairdressing, etc
- postal worker
- railway guard
- railway/coach catering staff
- taxi driver
- train driver

Other jobs where you travel

In these jobs, travel is just a means of getting from place to place to do your work. One advantage of many of these jobs is that there are also opportunities to do the work without *having* to be mobile, if you get tired of travelling, or if your circumstances change.

The important thing is to think first about the skills and interests you have. Then you can see what kind of jobs involve those skills and interests, and yet also give you the chance to be on the road, or out and about, for at least a part of your working day.

Selling and demonstrating jobs

- beauty consultant
- demonstrator for stores or exhibitions
- estate agent
- exhibitions organiser
- home economist (some work for electricity and gas supply companies)

- insurance salesperson
- sales representative
- technical salesperson

Practical work
- AA/RAC patrol person
- agricultural contractor
- agricultural engineer
- billposter
- builder
- carpenter
- carpet fitter
- central heating engineer
- chimney sweep
- construction worker
- electrician
- gas fitter
- landscaping contractor
- office machinery repairer
- plasterer
- plumber
- roofer
- scaffolder
- telephone engineer
- TV aerial erector
- TV repairs engineer
- windscreen/tyre fitter

Work in the social, educational and health services
- careers adviser
- charity fund-raiser
- district nurse
- education welfare officer

- escort (e.g. of children with special needs who need assistance to get to/from school on a daily basis, or who attend weekly boarding schools)
- general practitioner
- health visitor
- home carer
- midwife
- missionary
- peripatetic teacher (e.g. music, work with deaf children)
- school health service staff (e.g. nurse, audiologist, dental therapist)
- social worker
- veterinary surgeon
- voluntary service (overseas and home)

Emergency services
- ambulance service
- fire service
- police service

Inspecting and advisory work
- agricultural adviser
- environmental health officer
- factory inspector
- housing manager
- planning inspector
- property valuer
- trading standards officer

Professional work involving site work or visits, etc
- archaeologist
- architect
- building surveyor
- civil engineer

- forester
- geologist/geophysicist
- hydrographic surveyor
- land surveyor
- landscape architect
- structural engineer
- town and country planner

Miscellaneous

- entertainer/performer
- journalist
- photographic model
- politician
- press photographer
- travel agent or tour operator
- travelling farm secretary
- TV or film crew

TRAVEL & TOURISM

Travel and tourism is now a very large industry which provides services for tourists within Britain and for those going abroad on holidays. There is also a sizeable market created by business travel, sometimes with conferences to be organised and accommodation arrangements to be made. The work opportunities range from jobs for people leaving school with a few GCSEs or equivalent qualifications, to careers for graduates entering management training schemes to work in the industry.

Working in the United Kingdom
Tour operators

Tour operators arrange the transport, accommodation and leisure activities which make up package holidays. Usually these are packages for UK tourists going abroad, but some operators deal with holidays in Britain. Most tour operators are based in the London area. Firms offering British coach holidays are widespread throughout the UK.

Tour operators also develop new ideas for package holidays, and write, design and produce new brochures. They sell new packages to travel agents. Contracts with airlines and hotels have to be arranged.

Tour operators may deal directly with customers making reservations, as well as answering queries and dealing with problems. Getting into this area of work usually means starting from the bottom, even if you start as a graduate.

Travel agents

Travel agents act as a link between the client and the tour operators. Some agencies deal with a specific type of holiday, and most small agencies deal mainly with package holidays. The larger agencies try to meet a wide variety of demands from the public. This may include making individual travel arrangements, issuing travellers' cheques and foreign currency, and providing advice about visas and passports or information on insurance. The few larger chains have specialised departments at head office, e.g. business travel, small tours, accounts, personnel. Of these, Thomas Cook Limited, with a head office staff of about 2000, is the largest.

Selling package holidays and tours requires a wide knowledge of the main tourist areas, the different types of transportation, the products offered by tour operators and the various ways of making bookings. A first job could involve making reservations for air and ferry travel, booking package holidays, arranging hotel accommodation and dealing with foreign currency. Much of the work is done on computer. Don't forget that selling travel usually involves some weekend work, with time off during the week.

As most travel agencies are small, with perhaps three or four clerks and a manager, entry is normally through the Travel Training Company's own training, or by getting a job as a counter clerk. Experience of the industry and an outgoing personality are regarded as more important than formal qualifications, although three or four GCSEs may be asked for. Larger organisations, like Thomas Cook, have various graduate training schemes.

Desmond – travel agency clerk

‘ I suppose I did reasonably well at school, especially in maths and geography, but somehow going on to college or university just didn't appeal. So, when I was in year 11, I started thinking about jobs which I could go into with just good GCSEs. It had to be something which would give me a good training and chances for promotion. These days, most good jobs seem to need a degree! I had a couple of sessions with the careers adviser, which clarified my ideas a bit. Eventually the employment officer helped me to find a place as a trainee in a travel agency.

Most of the training was in the agency, but I had to attend a training centre as well. I learned a lot about the products I was selling (like package holidays, flights, ferry crossings), how to deal with people, issue tickets and use the computer systems. I even went on a trip abroad as part of the training.

After two years, I ended up with a National Vocational Qualification at level 3 – the equivalent of A levels – and I'm now working towards level 4. There are a lot of young people in the travel business, and you can get promoted to manager quite early in your career. It's not all that well paid, but you can get cheap holidays and travel as perks. Every year there are more exotic destinations in the brochures to learn about and – with a bit of luck – visit.

You need to like people to be a good travel agent, and you often have to work weekends and some late evenings. It's not as glamorous a job as you might think; you're just a salesperson really. When you start, there's a lot of unpacking parcels of brochures, making tea and such like, *but it soon gets more interesting. It can be very satisfying to help someone choose the right holiday for them, or to work out how to get from Glasgow to Zanzibar in the shortest possible time! I enjoy helping with the window displays too.*

Once you get to be a manager, it can be difficult to move any further up the ladder. I'll cross that bridge when I come to it. You can come into the business with a degree in travel and tourism, but most people start straight from school like I did. **,**

Tourist boards

There are four national tourist boards and the British Tourist Authority, all of whom promote holidays in the British Isles. There are also regional tourist boards concerned with promoting their own area, and local town, city and individual site facilities. Seasonal work may be available in local tourist information centres. This usually means evening and weekend work, and may well require knowledge of a foreign language.

Local authorities

Local authorities are involved in promoting tourism, to bring employment and trade to their area. **Tourism officers** work closely with others involved in the travel and tourism industry to:

■ publicise events and local facilities;
■ introduce new events to attract visitors;
■ advise councils on such matters as car parking and accommodation facilities in the area.

Tourism officers may have a background in the travel and tourism industry, or in leisure and recreation management or administration. Clerical and administrative posts in such departments may be available to people with good GCSEs or A levels, or equivalent qualifications.

Guides

Guides usually have a specialised knowledge of one area and provide a service for visitors, although some act as guides on coach tours, etc. They may take people round tourist attractions, or work in one important building like a cathedral or stately home. It is possible to train as a guide with tourist boards and local tourism authorities (courses are usually part-time), and with private guide agencies. The work is usually freelance and seasonal. A good conversational knowledge of one or two languages is very useful.

Working overseas

Many people are attracted to the travel business by the prospect of working in glamorous foreign holiday resorts. Competition is tough for vacancies and jobs may be seasonal, though winter work is increasing. The hours of work can be long, and the pressures great. If luggage is lost, clients are ill or flights are delayed, the courier or representative has to deal with it.

Couriers and representatives

Couriers travel with groups of holiday-makers, smoothing out problems as they go and pointing out places of historical or cultural interest. They need a good command of the languages of the countries they are going through, as well as the ability to get on well with people. **Representatives** stay in one resort, and liaise with hotel managers, sorting out day-to-day problems and perhaps selling day tours to clients.

In many companies, representatives are nationals of the country concerned, employed on the spot. Representatives recruited in this country are usually well over 20 and able to speak the language of the country they will work in.

QUALIFICATIONS AND TRAINING

There are no formal educational requirements, but most new entrants have at least three or four GCSEs at grade C, or an equivalent qualification. Some have A levels, an Advanced GNVQ, Higher National Diploma or degree. Useful subjects are maths and English, a foreign language, and perhaps geography. The majority of recruits start with the Travel Training Company's own training, while others begin with a college course. You can take specialist travel and tourism courses, or business studies courses with a travel and tourism component, at various colleges of further and higher education. These can be either full-time or part-time.

Full-time courses include:

- **Advanced GNVQ in Leisure and Tourism** – around four GCSEs at grade C for entry;
- **BTEC Higher National Diplomas** – one A level pass (plus a further subject studied to A level) and three other subjects at GCSE grade C/Advanced GNVQ/BTEC National Diploma for entry;
- **Degree courses** – a minimum of two A levels, together with supporting GCSEs, or qualifications equivalent to these, for entry. Brighton, Central Lancashire, Glasgow Caledonian, Humberside and North London universities offer four-year BA(Hons) degree courses in International Travel, Tourism and Leisure Management. There are some postgraduate courses.

There are also joint Travel Training Company/City & Guilds NVQs up to level 4, with units covering retail services, resort representatives, publicity, business travel, tour planning, tour guides, management and supervision. Qualifications are gained by a mixture of on-the-job and off-the-job training and assessment and distance learning. City & Guilds also offers a few specialist qualifications such as Farm-based Tourism and Visitor Attraction Practice. Most large travel and transport organisations – British Airways, for instance — run their own training schemes for employees. Regional tourist boards can advise on training of approved guides for sites in their area.

Adults: note that maturity and previous experience may mean that stated entry requirements can be relaxed.

FINDING A JOB

Contact travel agents, tourist agencies and attractions in your area. The Travel Training Company manages its own training, which includes business travel, tour operators and retail travel, and leads to NVQs up to level 3. Your local careers service should have details, or you can write to the Travel Training Company (see Further Information section), who will try to put you in touch with an employer in your area who is looking for a trainee, if you are unable to find one yourself.

You will find jobs advertised in the *Travel Trade Gazette*, *Travel Weekly* and the national or local press, but many of the posts advertised require some previous experience, either within tourism or another specialism (e.g. marketing).

Related areas of work

Some other areas of work include aspects of the travel and tourism industry:

- **Transport** – ferries, aircraft, trains, coaches, hire-cars;
- **Accommodation** – hotels, youth hostels, caravan sites, self-catering accommodation, holiday centres;
- **Food and drink** – restaurant meals, pubs, cafes, snack bars;
- **Recreation/entertainment** – zoos, museums, art galleries, historic houses, sports centres, theme parks;

- **Conference and exhibition organisation;**
- **Information** – brochures, booklets and posters.

See the relevant titles in the *Just the Job!* series for fuller details.

JOBS ON PASSENGER LINERS

A cruise liner is a floating hotel and, like a hotel, work goes on 24 hours a day. This means long and irregular hours for the crew. Few beginners find work on liners — it is usual for shipping lines to employ recruiting agencies to find crew members who already have experience in hotel work, or catering, retailing, beauty care and hairdressing, etc.

The attraction of work on a cruise liner is obvious. A luxurious ship gliding through warm tropical waters, mooring in exotic ports, moonlit evenings ... it all sounds very idyllic. Unfortunately, the crew have to work very hard to make all the delights of cruising available to the passengers! Also, the less desirable cabins are always allotted to the crew — below the waterline, near the engines, no porthole and you'll probably have to share. Many crew members are only allowed to mix with the passengers on business, so your social life could be limited.

Despite the disadvantages of this sort of life, cruise ship jobs are popular. Competition is fierce, and there is a very limited number of trainee posts for young entrants. This means that you need to have some relevant shore-based training or experience, possibly in one of the job areas mentioned above, or in nursing, secretarial work, childcare, the leisure/holiday business, or as a telephonist. Shipping companies usually expect a few years' relevant experience and the right sort of personality for the unusual lifestyle. The requirements listed below should only be taken as a guide, because different shipping lines will have different needs.

Deck and engineering officers and ratings

Recruitment and training for cruise ships is similar to that elsewhere in the merchant navy – see the book *In Uniform* in the *Just the Job!* series for fuller details.

Assistant purser

The purser's department on a cruise ship is responsible for the catering, administration of the ship, dealing with accounts, paying the crew, and passenger welfare and entertainment. The job is so big that sometimes a ship has **catering pursers** for the food side of the job and **administrative pursers** for the financial side.

Pursers' jobs, requiring a high level of qualification and experience, are few and far between and usually filled by promotion within. **Assistant pursers** require a fairly high standard of education and training, with secretarial and/or hotel and catering skills, perhaps fluency in a continental language, and experience in handling cash and reception work. You need to be good at dealing with people – both staff and passengers. Most people start as assistant pursers between the ages of 21 and 35, although older applicants are recruited for certain positions.

Children's host/hostess

Children's hosts are responsible to the purser for the children on board, and for organising games and entertainments. Relevant experience is required; some employers require their children's hosts to be qualified infant or junior teachers.

Qualified **nursery nurses** often work with or under the supervision of the children's host.

Entertainment officer/cruise director/ social host/hostess

Actual duties and level of responsibility may vary with the job title. The person in this job plays host to passengers, especially old and lonely people, and organises general passenger entertainment. He or she should have a lively personality, stamina and relevant experience in the leisure/recreation field, and is often required to be able to sing, dance or entertain in some way.

Telephonist

Telephonists maintain a 24-hour service on the ship-to-shore telephone, and should have British Telecom training and several years' experience – ideally of a hotel switchboard. A working knowledge of European languages is useful.

Hairdresser/beauty therapist

These are usually not employed directly by a shipping line, but by a firm with ship-based salons, such as the maritime division of the Steiner Group. Only very experienced and well-trained therapists and hairdressers will be able to get work on a ship.

Retail work

Various firms, such as Allders International, run shops on cruise liners, selling luxury and duty-free goods. Shop staff are employed by the firms which supply the goods, and not by the shipping companies themselves.

Medical staff

Cruise ships have a resident **nurse**, a **doctor**, and often a quali-fied **pharmacist.** Nurses should have the RGN (Registered General Nurse) qualification with post-training experience in as many branches of nursing as possible.

Croupier

Cruise ships often have a casino where croupiers are needed. The croupier runs each individual game, taking in the bets and paying out the winnings. The casino concession will be run by an outside concern.

Printer

Cruise ships usually produce an on-board newspaper to keep the guests entertained and aware of the programme of events each day. A printer is required to compose the newspaper layout and to print it. To get this type of work, you would preferably need to have experience of desk-top publishing techniques and a flexible approach to work.

Cinema projectionist

Experienced and competent projectionists are needed to operate equipment in ship cinemas. Some lines may require operators to be members of an appropriate union.

Other occupations

These include carpenters and plumbers, photographers, massage therapists, fitness instructors, musicians and dancers and maintenance and repair staff for gambling machines.

FINDING EMPLOYMENT

If you have some relevant experience, write to potential employers asking for information about vacancies. Individual shipping lines should be able to give information about contracting firms providing services for them. Remember that, as well as cruise ships, there are short-haul ferries which need catering, domestic, office and shop staff. This work is often temporary and seasonal, however, as the demand for crossings is much greater in the holiday season.

Overseas Jobs Express, which may be in your local careers service or public library, is a good source of information about agencies and vacancies for work on cruise liners.

AIRLINE STAFF

Air cabin crew

> Air cabin crew are responsible for attending to the safety, needs and comfort of passengers during flights. Although the job has a glamorous image, it is responsible and demanding work.

Many young people dream of becoming an **air steward** or **hostess** when they leave school, seeing it as a glamorous life, flying to exotic places. The flying and the exotic aspects are there, but, as anyone who has flown will know, much of the job is also routine and hard work. Cabin crew must appear friendly and sympathetic to anyone needing help, advice, reassurance, sympathy or even, at times, firm persuasion. Passengers may be of all ages, nationalities, religions, occupations and social backgrounds.

The main responsibility of the air cabin crew is the safety of their passengers, both in normal conditions and in emergencies. They have to ensure that all passengers are aware of the safety procedures, making general announcements and sometimes passing on specific messages from the captain. Other principal duties include serving meals and drinks, allowing for special diets and health requirements. Meals are mainly pre-packed but may need heating before service. In a small galley and the narrow gangways of an aircraft, it is not easy to prepare and serve meals and drinks to a large number of passengers!

The work entails unusual hours: duty rosters normally include

early morning and late night flights. Although this is an interesting job offering variety and the chance to travel, it is also very strenuous and demanding. Opportunities exist for promotion to **Senior Steward/Senior Stewardess**. Both men and women can continue in service until normal retirement age, which is usually 55.

GETTING STARTED

Cabin crew are normally recruited by airlines between the ages of 19 and 30. Competition for openings is very keen. At the moment, there is very little recruitment. A pleasant personality and high standards of physical fitness and appearance are needed.

Applicants must pass a medical examination and meet fairly stringent requirements regarding height and weight. Some companies permit glasses or contact lenses to be worn, providing unaided vision is up to the required standard. You may also need good colour vision for some firms.

Entry qualifications vary between airlines, but, generally, a good educational standard is looked for, and some higher grade GCSEs (or their equivalent) are desirable. Applicants should be able to swim, and proficiency in a modern language is a decided asset. Useful experience includes catering, nursing and any activity involving service to the public.

Selection starts at the application form stage – apply in writing or by telephone, to the airline of your choice, for an application form. A completed form and recent photograph are submitted, and selected applicants are called for a preliminary interview. Success at this stage is often followed by a further interview and tests.

TRAINING

Training begins with about five to six weeks at a training school and is usually carried out in an airline environment, including a full-size mock-up aircraft cabin. The training includes lectures, visits, discussions and video presentations covering all aspects of the eventual duties of cabin crew members. These include safety and emergency procedures, presentation of meals and drinks, first aid, currency exchange, customer relations and customs and immigration regulations. After this induction course, trainees become qualified cabin crew members. Advanced training follows on the air routes and continues during the first year, which is a probationary period.

Passenger service assistants

An airline's image with the travelling public, and the smooth running of its operations, depends very much on the **ground passenger service staff**, now sometimes referred to as **customer service agents**. Passenger service assistants/customer service agents sometimes work in city air terminals but, more usually, at airports. They deal with passengers both face-to-face and on the phone. They check passengers in, allocate seats, assemble, escort, advise, assist and control passengers together with their baggage – taking particular care of families with young children, unaccompanied children, elderly and invalid passengers and VIPs.

ENTRY AND TRAINING

Applicants must be over 18; the preferred age range in some airlines is 20-27. A good standard of general education is required, preferably with some higher grade GCSEs or their equivalent. Useful subjects are English language, mathematics, geography and a modern language. Experience in clerical/reception work, nursing or dealing with the public is an advantage, and conversational ability in a foreign language is a decided asset.

Each airline used to train its own staff, but nowadays airlines often subcontract this function to handling agents, such as Gatwick Handling, Service Air, etc. Programmes of induction vary, but would include lectures, visits, practical exercises and on-the-job instruction by experienced staff.

PROSPECTS

For those with ability and experience, there are opportunities for promotion to more senior positions in passenger service and other departments, including some at overseas stations on the airlines' routes.

DRIVING JOBS

This section covers driving lorries, buses, coaches and taxis and driving instructing. There are all sorts of rules and regulations about the different jobs, so read carefully before making decisions. For most of these jobs you have to be over 21 before you can get the necessary licence.

Lorry driver

Lorry driving is a well-paid job which seems to offer a lot of freedom and variety. Travelling around the country, and even going abroad, seems – to some people – to offer a better life than working in a shop, office or factory; and drivers don't have a supervisor watching them work all the time!

But, of course, there are drawbacks. The awkward hours which driving often involves don't suit everyone, and can mean being away from home or working at night. Working conditions, in bad weather especially, can be difficult and dangerous. Not every journey will take you somewhere new and exciting – you may cover the same delivery route day in, day out.

You need to be fit and reasonably strong to drive lorries, with good eyesight. You must be able to work alone, concentrate for long periods, and cope with emergencies if they arise.

You are responsible for:

■ loading and unloading the cargo;
■ planning and keeping records of routes;
■ maintaining the vehicle while on the road;

- customs and excise checks on the cargo;
- recording hours worked and breaks taken.

Drivers can work for haulage firms, industrial or retail companies, or they may own their own lorries and be self-employed. Both men and women can become lorry drivers.

TRAINING TO DRIVE LORRIES

You can learn to drive as soon as you are seventeen. The ordinary test (Category B) permits you to drive a vehicle with not more than eight seats and weighing up to 3.5 tonnes. You can then progress to heavier vehicles, up to 7.5 tonnes, by taking a further test.

- Over the age of 21 and with a clean licence, you can apply for your LGV (Large Goods Vehicle) licence, enabling you to drive lorries of up to 12 tonnes. A further test enables you to drive the extremely large articulated lorries.
- Training for the LGV licence could be as an employee with a large firm which employs its own instructors, with a firm belonging to a group training scheme in which several firms share instructors, or by going to a driving school which has a special industrial scheme to train LGV drivers.
- It is also possible to train as an LGV driver in the armed forces.
- The Young Drivers Scheme, which trained young drivers so that they were ready to take their LGV test at 21, has been revised and will be running as soon as the changes have been approved. Contact the Road Haulage and Distribution Training Council for further details.
- Modern Apprenticeships in Road Haulage and Distribution may be available in your area. Contact your local Training and Enterprise Council for further information.

Adults who have been unemployed for over six months may

be eligible to cover the groundwork for a specialised driving licence, e.g. for a fork-lift truck, while on a Training for Work placement. Ask at your local Jobcentre/Employment Service about possibilities.

Bus driver

To be a bus driver you must have a passenger-carrying vehicle driver's licence (PCV). To get one of these you will have to go on a bus or coach driving course and take a test, having already passed your ordinary (category B) driving test and got a provisional PCV licence. You will normally have to be 21 or over — although it may be possible to drive a minibus on short routes at age 18. Your driving licence must be free of endorsements for serious motoring offences. You need to be in good health, with good eyesight (glasses allowed), and have enough mechanical sense to know if the bus is developing a fault. You must also be prepared to work irregular hours, early in the morning, late at night and at weekends. Some employers have height regulations, and a good time-keeping record is useful!

The length of training depends on your previous experience, but it will be several weeks before you find yourself on the road with a bus.

The job involves taking fares, giving change, dealing with passengers' enquiries, checking the day's takings, as well as driving the bus, as few buses outside London have conductors. The driver is therefore responsible for making sure that bus company regulations are observed and that difficult passengers such as late-night drunks and rowdy school children are dealt with firmly. Some bus drivers become **inspectors**.

Coach driver

The basic requirements for a coach driver are much the same as for a bus driver. You must be over 21 and have a passenger-carrying vehicle licence.

Coach driving can be more varied than bus driving. You could drive a coach for a small company doing local school bus trips, outings and some scheduled services; you could work for a national company doing long distance services, or you could work for a coach tour operator doing tours of Britain or the Continent. It is possible for a driver to obtain an operator's licence and start their own business with their own coach or coaches.

Coach driving, particularly for tour operators, is a responsible job. You may be away from base for some time, so the mechanical state of your vehicle is very much your concern. The loading, unloading and refuelling of the coach will be part of your job, as well as possibly acting as guide and helper to the passengers. You might have to give a commentary on a sightseeing tour. Coach companies are mostly relatively small, and don't usually train their own drivers, so you would have to get a PCV licence before finding a job. For driving on a coach tour you would have to be an experienced driver already.

Bus and Coach Training Ltd award National Vocational Qualifications in driving and customer care at NVQ level 2, plus a level 3 qualification for instructors.

Taxi and hire–car driver

Taxi and hire-car drivers have to be licensed by the local authority of the area in which they work. **Taxis** are more tightly controlled, but have the advantage that they can wait on official cab ranks and ply for hire on the streets with a sign on the taxi. Drivers may own their own cabs or drive for a fleet and pay the owner a percentage of takings. **Mini–cabs** or **private hire vehicles** can only work through telephone or radio-control bookings.

The rules and regulations can vary from area to area. In London, for example, hackney carriage drivers must be over 21, pass a medical test and be familiar with all the thousands of streets and major buildings within six miles of Charing Cross. Out of London things are less demanding. Normally you must have a current driving licence, undergo a police check and a medical test, be tested in your knowledge of your area, have your vehicle inspected for mechanical condition and suitability for use as a taxi or hire-car, and have the right kind of insurance. There is a waiting list in many areas for drivers who would like to run a taxi. Consult your local authority for details of the licensing rules in your area.

Driving instructor

To teach people to drive professionally – that is, in return for payment - it is necessary to be on the Register of Approved Driving Instructors of the Driving Standards Agency or to be a trainee licensed to give instruction. To get on this register or become a licensed trainee, you must have held a full (not provisional) driving licence for at least four years out of the last six. This means you must be at least 21 and, in practice, very few instructors are approved under the age of 25. You must not have been disqualified from driving during the last four years, and you must be a 'fit and proper person' to have your name entered on the register. All convictions are taken into account under this heading, though not if they are regarded as being 'spent' in terms of the Rehabilitation of Offenders Act. For full approved status, a written and two practical tests must be passed. Private training courses are available. Both the training and the tests cost money. Even when qualified, an instructor is occasionally assessed by the Agency.

Driving instructors may work for driving schools, operate under a franchise, or have their own business using their own car. A good instructor enjoys working with people of all kinds – including the very nervous! He or she must be able to give clear instructions, be patient and tactful, and have very good concentration and quick reactions. Remember, not all learner drivers are perfect pupils – instructing is a very demanding job. To build up a successful business you must be prepared to work odd hours, to fit in with pupils' free time. Evening and weekend work is very common.

Other opportunities

It is also possible for drivers with suitable experience to become **instructors** of LGV, FLT (fork-lift truck) and PCV drivers, or motorcyclists. People with a wide range of different driving experience can become **driving examiners**, trained and employed by the Driving Standards Agency. Driving examiners must meet very stringent requirements and be of minimum age 25, though most would be considerably older on first appointment. They have to have good eyesight and health, be good communicators, and to pass a one-and-a-half hour driving test and interview before being selected for training.

FOR FURTHER INFORMATION

GENERAL

Hotel and Catering International Management Association (HCIMA) – 191 Trinity Road, London SW17 7HN. Tel: 0181 672 4251.

Hospitality Training Foundation – International House, High Street, Ealing, London W5 5DB. Tel: 0181 579 2400.

Careers in Catering and Hotel Management, published by Kogan Page.

Careers and Training in Hotels, Catering and Tourism, by Roy Hayter, published by Butterworth-Heinemann.

Running your own Catering Company, by J. Ridgway, published by Kogan Page.

Working in Food and Drink, published by COIC.

Working in Hotels and Catering, published by COIC.

COOKING AND FOOD PREPARATION

Cookery and Food Association (CFA) – 1 Victoria Parade, by 331 Sandycombe Road, Richmond, Surrey TW9 3NB. Tel: 0181 948 3870.

Vegetarian Society of the UK Ltd – Parkdale, Dunham Road, Altrincham, Cheshire WA14 4QG. Tel: 0161 928 0793.

SERVING FOOD AND DRINK

Academy of Food and Wine Service – Burgoine House, 8 Lower Teddington Road, Kingston upon Thames, Surrey KT1 4ER. Tel: 0181 943 1011.

Brewers and Licensed Retailers Association – 42 Portman Square, London W1H 0BB. Tel: 0171 486 4831.

British Institute of Innkeeping – Wessex House, 80 Park Street, Camberley, Surrey GU15 3PT. Tel: 01276 684449.

Wine and Spirit Education Trust – Five Kings House, 1 Queen Street Place, London EC4R 1QS. Tel: 0171 236 3551.

Running Your Own Pub by Elven Money, published by Kogan Page.

Leisure and Hospitality Management, an AGCAS careers booklet for graduates, available from the Central Services Unit, Crawford House, Precinct Centre, Manchester M13 9EP. Tel: 0161 273 4233.

THE FOOD INDUSTRY

Food and Drink Industry Training Organisation – 6 Catherine Street, London WC2B 5JJ. Tel: 0171 836 2460.

Institute of Food Science and Technology (UK) – 5 Cambridge Court, 210 Shepherd's Bush Road, London W6 7NL. Tel: 0171 603 6316.

Institute of Grocery Distribution – Careers Information Service, Letchmore Heath, Watford, WD2 8DQ. Tel: 01923 857141. The Institute publishes a list of food manufacturers.

Meat Training Council – Winterhill House, Snowdon Drive, Milton Keynes MK6 1YY. Tel: 01908 231062.

National Dairy Council – 5–7 John Princes Street, London W1M 0AP. Tel: 0171 499 7822.

BAKING AND CONFECTIONERY

Federation of Bakers (for plant bakeries) – 20 Bedford Square, London WC1B 3HF. Tel: 0171 580 4252 for a list of members.

National Association of Master Bakers (for craft bakeries) – 21 Baldock Street, Ware, Hertfordshire SG12 9DH. Tel: 01920 468061 – queries on qualifications and training to 01225 864500. Produces a useful list of the colleges offering courses, and booklets on career opportunities in plant and craft baking.

The weekly publication, *British Baker*, is a useful source of information about the industry, and carries a vacancy list.

BUTCHERY

Association of Meat Inspectors – 44 Parkfield Road, Taunton, Somerset TA1 4SF.

Meat and Livestock Commission – Marketing Department, PO Box 44, Winterhill House, Snowdon Drive, Milton Keynes, MK6 1YY. Can provide leaflets and posters about working in the butchery business.

Meat Training Council – PO Box 141, Winterhill House, Snowdon Drive, Milton Keynes, MK6 1YY. Tel: 01908 231062. Can provide information on the new Modern Apprenticeships in Meat.

Worshipful Company of Butchers – Butchers' Hall, 87 Bartholemew Close, London EC1A 7EB. Tel: 0171 606 4106.

What's What in Meat Education and Training- a guide to education and training for the meat industry, 1994, compiled by Dr Bernard Hawes and published by the Meat Training Council (address above). This guide may be available for reference in school, college or careers centre libraries.

FOOD SCIENCE AND TECHNOLOGY

Food and Drink Federation – 6 Catherine Street, London WC2B 5JJ. Tel: 0171 836 2460.

Food and Drink Industry Training Organisation – 6 Catherine Street, London WC2B 5JJ.

Institute of Food Science and Technology of the UK – 5 Cambridge Court, 210 Shepherd's Bush Road, London W6 7NL. Tel: 0171 603 6316.

HOME ECONOMICS

Institute of Home Economics – Hobart House, 40 Grosvenor Place, London SW1X 7AE. Tel: 0171 823 1109.

National Association of Teachers of Home Economics and Technology – Hamilton House, Mabledon Place, London WC1H 9BJ. Tel: 0171 387 1441.

The Home Economist is the bi-monthly journal of the Institute of Home Economics, and *Modus* is the journal of NATHE.

Look in the phone book for your local and regional tourist board
addresses, and also for travel agents and tour operators.

Chartered Institute of Transport – 80 Portland Place, London
W1N 4DP. Tel: 0171 636 9952.

English Tourist Board – Training and Business Support,
Thames Tower, Blacks Road, London W6 9EL. Tel: 0181 563
3219. The Tourist Board offers free careers leaflets.

Institute of Travel and Tourism – 113 Victoria Street, St.
Albans, Hertfordshire AL1 3TJ. Tel: 01727 854395. The
Institute produces a careers pack – ring for details.

Travel Training Company – The Cornerstone, The Broadway,
Woking, Surrey GU21 5AR. Tel: 01483 727321. Enclose a
large stamped addressed envelope for their comprehensive
information pack.

Careers in the Travel Industry, published by Kogan Page.
Careers on the move, published by The Chartered Institute of
Transport, 1995 (available from the above address.)
Tourism – an AGCAS graduate careers information booklet.
Available for consultation in many careers centres, or from
CSU, Crawford House, Precinct Centre, Manchester M13 9EP.
Travel Trade Directory – produced by Travel Trade Gazette –
contains useful addresses and is often available in public libraries.
Working in Tourism, published by COIC.

PASSENGER LINERS
This list is not comprehensive: there are many other shipping lines
and recruitment agencies (inclusion in this list is not a
recommendation):

Allders International (Ships) – (for retailers) 84–98
Southampton Road, Eastleigh, Hampshire SO50 5ZF. Tel:
01703 644599.

Cunard Line Ltd. – Fleet Personnel Department, South Western
House, Canute Road, Southampton SO14 3NR. Tel: 01703
229933.

P & O Cruises Ltd. – Fleet Personnel Department, Richmond House, Terminus Terrace, Southampton SO14 3PN. Send stamped self-addressed envelope for brochure *Seagoing opportunities with P & O Cruises* for general information, or send letter with cv and stamped addressed envelope for more specific enquiries.

Southern Games – (for trained and experienced croupiers only) 202 Fulham Road, Chelsea, London SW10 9NB. Tel: 0171 352 0034.

Steiner Group Ltd. – (for hairdressers, beauty therapists, etc) Maritime Division, 57–65 The Broadway, Stanmore, Middlesex HA7 4DU. Tel: 0181 954 6121.

VIP International – VIP House, 17 Charing Cross Road, London WC2H 0EP. Tel: 0171 930 0541 – recruit bar staff, waiters, chefs, etc.

COMMERCIAL AIRLINES

Air 2000 – Tower Block, Manchester International Airport, Manchester M22 5EP. Tel: 0161 489 3840.

Air League Educational Trust – 4 Hamilton Place, London W1V 0BQ. Tel: 0171 491 0471.

British Airline Pilots' Association – 81 New Road, Harlington, Hayes, Middlesex UB3 5BG. Tel: 0181 759 9331.

British Airways plc – Pilot Recruitment, Meadowbank, PO Box 59, Hounslow, Middlesex TW5 9QX. Tel: 0181 564 1013.

British Airways plc – Air Cabin Crew Recruitment, PO Box 59, Hounslow, Middlesex TW5 9QX. Tel: 0181 564 1449.

British Helicopter Advisory Board – The Graham Suite, West Entrance, Fairoaks Airport, Chobham, Surrey GU24 8HX. Tel: 01276 856100.

Bristow Helicopters (Eastern) Ltd – Redhill Aerodrome, Redhill, Surrey RH1 5JZ. Tel: 01737 822353.

British Midland – Donington Hall, Castle Donington, Derby DE7 2SB. Tel: 01332 810741.

Britannia Airways – Recruitment and Training Centre, East Midlands Airport, Castle Donington, Derby DE7 2SA. Tel: 01332 812469.

Civil Aviation Authority – Aviation House, Gatwick Airport South, West Sussex RH6 0YR. Tel: 01293 573590/573556. The CAA publishes the guide *Professional Pilots' Licences*.

Virgin Atlantic – Ashdown House, High Street, Crawley, West Sussex RH10 1DQ. Tel: 01293 562345.

Flight Directory of British Aviation – Kelly's Directories: available in most public libraries.

Sponsorship schemes are likely to be advertised in the magazines *Flight International* and *Pilot*.

DRIVING JOBS

You will find addresses of coach operators – many of whom now run scheduled bus services – and road haulage and car hire firms in *Yellow Pages*.

Bus and Coach Training Ltd – Regency House, 43 High Street, Rickmansworth, Hertfordshire WD3 1ET. Tel: 01923 896607.

Chartered Institute of Transport in the UK – 80 Portland Place, London W1N 4DP. Tel: 0171 636 9952.

Confederation of Passenger Transport – Sardinia House, 52 Lincoln's Inn Fields, London EC2A 3LZ. Tel: 0171 831 7546.

Driving Standards Agency – Stanley House, 56 Talbot Street, Nottingham NG1 5GU. Tel: 01159 557600. (Publishes *Your Road to becoming a Driving Instructor*, which includes an application form.)

Road Haulage Association – Roadway House, 35 Monument Hill, Weybridge, Surrey KT13 8RN. Tel: 01932 841515.

Road Haulage and Distribution Training Council – Suite C, Shenley Hall, Rectory Lane, Shenley, Radlett, Hertfordshire WD7 9AN. Tel: 01923 858461.

Road Transport Industry Training Board – Centrex, High Ercall, Telford, Shropshire TF6 6RB. Tel: 01952 770441. (Can provide information about LGV training centres, etc.)

Road Transport, a Careers in Focus video. Ask at your local Careers Centre.

Working in Passenger Transport, published by COIC.

660